Editor

Fred L. Israel

VOLUME 5

Theodore Roosevelt 1901 – Herbert Hoover 1933

Grolier Educational
SHERMAN TURNPIKE, DANBURY, CONNECTICUT

The publisher gratefully acknowledges permission from the sources to reproduce photos that appear on the cover.

Volume 1
J. Adams – New York Historical Society
J. Monroe – Library of Congress

Volume 2
J. K. Polk; A. Jackson; J. Tyler – Library of Congress
J. Q. Adams – National Archives

Volume 3
U. S. Grant – National Archives
A. Johnson; Z. Taylor – Library of Congress

Volume 4
B. Harrison; W. McKinley; J. A. Garfield – Library of Congress

Volume 5
H. Hoover; W. G. Harding – Library of Congress
T. Roosevelt – National Archives

Volume 6
D. D. Eisenhower – Library of Congress
L. B. Johnson – White House

Volume 7
B. Clinton – The White House
R. Reagan – Bush/Reagan Committee
G. Bush – Cynthia Johnson, The White House

Volume 8
T. Roosevelt – National Archives
B. Clinton – The White House

Published 1997 exclusively for the school and library market by Grolier Educational
Sherman Turnpike, Danbury, Connecticut

Set: ISBN 0-7172-7642-2
Volume 5: ISBN 0-7172-7647-3

Library of Congress number:
The presidents.
p. cm.
Contents: v. 1. 1789–1825 (Washington–Monroe) — v. 2. 1825–1849 (Adams–Polk)
v. 3. 1849–1877 (Taylor–Grant) — v. 4. 1877–1901 (Hayes–McKinley) — v. 5.1901–1933 (T. Roosevelt–Hoover)
v. 6. 1933–1969 (F. D. Roosevelt–L. B. Johnson) — v. 7. 1969–1997 (Nixon–Clinton)
v. 8. Documents, suggested reading, charts, tables, appendixes

1. Presidents – United States – Juvenile literature.
[1. Presidents.] 96-31491
E176.1.P9175 1997 CIP
973.099 — dc20 AC

For information, address the publisher
Grolier Educational, Sherman Turnpike, Danbury, Connecticut 06816

Printed in the United States of America

Cover design by Smart Graphics

Volume Five

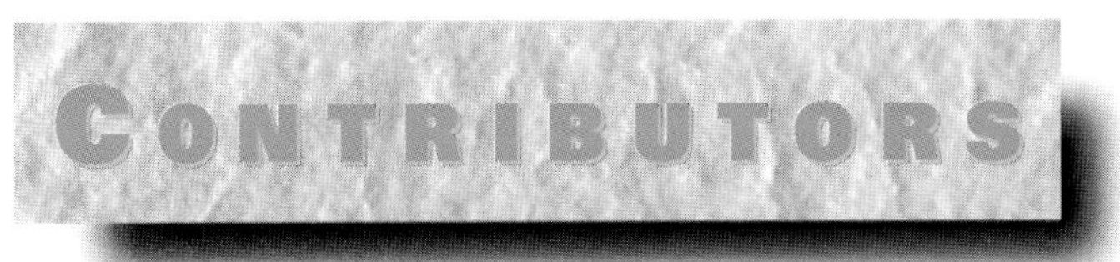

EDITOR

Fred L. Israel received his Ph.D. from Columbia University. He has written several books for young adults including *Franklin D. Roosevelt, Henry Kissinger,* and *Know Your Government: The FBI.* Dr. Israel is also the editor of *History of American Presidential Elections, 1789–1968, The Chief Executive: Inaugural Addresses of the Presidents from George Washington to Lyndon Johnson,* and *The State of the Union Messages of the Presidents of the United States.* His most recent book is *Running for President, The Candidates and Their Images,* a two-volume work with Arthur M. Schlesinger, Jr. and David J. Frent.

Dr. Israel is Professor, Department of History, The City College of the City University of New York.

CONTRIBUTORS

Donald C. Bacon is a Washington-based journalist specializing in the presidency and Congress. He served as staff writer of *The Wall Street Journal* and assistant managing editor of *U.S. News and World Report.* A former Congressional Fellow, he is the author of *Rayburn: A Biography* and *Congress and You.* He is coeditor of *The Encyclopedia of the United States Congress.*

Hendrik Booraem V received his Ph.D. from The Johns Hopkins University. He taught social studies at Strom Thurmond High School, South Carolina, for many years. He has been Adjunct Professor at Rutgers University, Camden, Alvernia College, Lehigh University, and the State University of New York at Purchase. Dr. Booraem is the author of *The Formation of the Republican Party in New York: Politics and Conscience in the Antebellum North, The Road to Respectability: James A. Garfield and His World, 1844–1852,* and *The Provincial: Calvin Coolidge and His World, 1885–1895.*

Thomas Bracken received his B.A. and M.A., summa cum laude, from The City College of the City University of New York. He is currently enrolled in the doctoral program there, and he is Adjunct Professor of History.

David Burner received his Ph.D. from Columbia University. He is Professor of American History at the State University of New York at Stony Brook. Among Dr. Burner's many publications are *John F. Kennedy and a New Generation, The Torch is Passed: The Kennedy Brothers and American Liberalism* (with Thomas R. West) and *The Politics of Provincialism: The Democratic Party in Transition, 1918–1932.* He is also the coauthor of *Firsthand America: A History of the United States.*

Gary Cohn received his M.A. in Popular Culture Studies from Bowling Green State University in 1980 and has completed course work towards the doctorate in American History at the State University of New York at Stony Brook. As an Adjunct Professor he has taught history at The City College of the City University of New York and creative writing and composition at the C.W. Post campus of Long Island University.

Richard Nelson Current is University Distinguished Professor of History, Emeritus, at the University of North Carolina, Greensboro and former President of the Southern Historical Association. Among Dr. Current's many books are *Speaking of Abraham Lincoln: The Man and His Meaning for Our Times, Lincoln and the First Shot, The Lincoln Nobody Knows, Lincoln the President: Last Full Measure,* and with T. Harry Williams and Frank Freidel, *American History: A Survey.*

James B. Gardner received his Ph.D. from Vanderbilt University. He has been Deputy Executive Director of the American Historical Association since 1986 and Acting Executive Director of that organization since 1994. Dr. Gardner was with the American Association for State and Local History from 1979 to 1986, where he served in a variety of capacities, including Director of Education and Special Programs. Among his many publications is *A Historical Guide to the United States.*

Anne-Marie Grimaud received her B.A. from the Sorbonne, Paris and her M.A. from the State University of New York at Stony Brook, where she is currently enrolled in the doctoral program in American History.

Douglas Kinnard graduated from the United States Military Academy and served in Europe during World War II. He also served in Korea and Vietnam and retired as Brigadier General. He then received his Ph.D. from Princeton University. Dr. Kinnard is Professor Emeritus, University of Vermont and was Chief of Military History, U.S. Army. Among Dr. Kinnard's books are *Ike 1890–1990: A Pictorial History, President Eisenhower and Strategy Management: A Study in Defense Politics,* and *Maxwell Taylor and The American Experience in Vietnam.*

Robert A. Raber received his J.D. from the Law School, University of California, Berkeley. He retired from law practice and received his M.A. from The City College of the City University of New York, where he is enrolled in the doctoral program.

Donald A. Ritchie received his Ph.D. from the University of Maryland. Dr. Ritchie is on the Executive Committee of the American Historical Association, and he has been Associate Historian, United States Senate for 20 years. Among his many publications are *Press Gallery: Congress and the Washington Correspondents, The Young Oxford Companion to the Congress of the United States,* and *Oxford Profiles of American Journalists.*

Robert A. Rutland is Professor of History Emeritus, University of Virginia. He was editor in chief of *The Papers of James Madison* for many years, and he was coordinator of bicentennial programs at the Library of Congress from 1969 to 1971. Dr. Rutland is the author of many books including *Madison's Alternatives: The Jeffersonian Republicans and the Coming of War, 1805–1812, James Madison and the Search for Nationhood, James Madison: The Founding Father,* and *The Presidency of James Madison.* He is editor of *James Madison and the American Nation, 1751–1836: An Encyclopedia.*

Raymond W. Smock received his Ph.D. from the University of Maryland. He was involved with the Booker T. Washington Papers Project for many years and was coeditor from 1975 to 1983. He was Historian, Office of the Bicentennial, U.S. House of Representatives. In 1983, he was appointed as the first Director of the Office of the Historian of the U.S. House of Representatives. Among the major publications of that office are *The Biographical Directory of the United States Congress, 1774–1989, Black Americans in Congress, 1877–1989,* and *Women in Congress, 1917–1990.*

Darren D. Staloff received his Ph.D. from Columbia University, and he was a Post-Doctoral Fellow at the Institute of Early American History and Culture. He has taught at the College of Staten Island, Columbia University, and the College of William and Mary. Dr. Staloff is currently Assistant Professor of American History, The City College of The City University of New York. He is the author of *The Making of an American Thinking Class: Intellectuals and Intelligentsia in Puritan Massachusetts.*

John Stern received his M.A. from the State University of New York at Stony Brook, where he is enrolled in the doctoral program. His thesis is on Eugene McCarthy and the Presidential Campaign of 1968.

Edmund B. Sullivan received his Ed.D. from Fitchburg State College. He was Principal, New Hampton Community School, New Hampshire, and he taught at the North Adams and Newton public schools in Massachusetts. Dr. Sullivan was Professor at American International College and University of Hartford, and he was the founding Director and Curator of the Museum of American Political Life, West Hartford Connecticut. He is the author of *American Political Ribbons and Ribbon Badges, 1828–1988, American Political Badges and Medalets, 1789–1892,* and *Collecting Political Americana.*

Linda S. Vertrees received her B.A. in History from Western Illinois University and her M.A. in Library Science from the University of Chicago. She has written several annotated lists of suggested readings including the one for *The Holocaust, A Grolier Student Library.*

Thomas R. West received his Ph.D. from the Columbia University. He is Associate Professor, Department of History, Catholic University. He is coauthor, with David Burner, of *The Torch is Passed: The Kennedy Brothers and American Liberalism* and *Column Right: Conservative Journalists in the Service of Nationalism.*

No branch of the federal government caused the authors of the Constitution as many problems as did the Executive. They feared a strong chief of state. After all, the American Revolution was, in part, a struggle against the King of England and the powerful royal governors. Surprisingly though, much power was granted to the president of the United States who is responsible only to the people. This was the boldest feature of the new Constitution. The president has varied duties. Above all, he must take care that the laws be faithfully executed. And also according to the Constitution, the president:

- is the commander in chief of the armed forces;
- has the power to make treaties with other nations (with the Senate's consent);
- appoints Supreme Court Justices and other members of the federal courts, ambassadors to other countries, department heads, and other high officials (all with the Senate's consent);
- signs into law or vetoes bills passed by Congress;
- calls special sessions of Congress in times of emergency.

In some countries, the power to lead is inherited. In others, men seize power through force. But in the United States, the people choose the nation's leader. The power of all the people to elect the president was not stated in the original Constitution. This came later. The United States is the first nation to have an elected president—and a president with a stated term of office. Every four years since the adoption of the Constitution in 1789, the nation has held a presidential election. Elections have been held even during major economic disruptions and wars. Indeed, these elections every four years are a vivid reminder of our democratic roots.

Who can vote for president of the United States? The original Constitution left voting qualifications to the states. At first, the states limited voting to white and very few black men who owned a certain amount of property. It was argued that only those with an economic or commercial interest in the nation should have a say in who could run the government. After the Civil War (1861–1865), the Fourteenth (1868) and Fifteenth (1870) Amendments to the Constitution guaranteed the vote to all men over the age of 21. The guarantee was only in theory. The Nineteenth Amendment (1920) extended the right to vote to women. The Nineteenth Amendment was a victory of the woman's suffrage movement which had worked for many years to achieve this goal. In 1964, the Twenty-fourth Amendment abolished poll taxes—a fee paid before a citizen was allowed to vote. This tax had kept many poor people, both black and white, from voting in several Southern states. And, the Twenty-sixth Amendment (1971) lowered the voting age to 18. (See Volume 8 for the complete text of the Constitution.)

In 1965, Congress passed the Voting Rights Act; it was renewed in 1985. This law, which carried out the requirements of the Fifteenth Amendment, made it illegal to interfere with anyone's right to vote. It forbade the use of literacy tests and, most important, the law mandated that federal voter registrars be sent into counties where less than 50 percent of the voting age population (black and white) was registered. This assumed that there must be serious barriers based on prejudice if so few had registered to vote. Those who had prevented African Americans from voting through fear and threat of violence now had to face the force of the federal government. Immediately, the number of African American voters in Southern states jumped dramatically from about 35 percent to 65 percent. In 1970, 1975, and 1982, Congress added amendments to the Voting Rights Act which helped other minorities such as Hispanics, Asians, Native Americans, and

Eskimos. For example, states must provide bilingual ballots in counties in which 5 percent or more of the population does not speak or read English. Today any citizen over the age of 18 has the right to vote in a presidential election. Many would argue that this is not only a right but also an obligation. However, all states deny the right to vote to anyone who is in prison.

Who can be president of the United States? There are formal constitutional requirements: one must be a "natural born citizen," at least 35 years old, and a resident of the United States for 14 years. The Constitution refers to the president as "he." It was probably beyond the thought process of the Founding Fathers that a woman, or a man who was not white, would ever be considered. The Twenty-second Amendment (1951), which deals with term limitations, uses "person" in referring to the president, recognizing that a woman could serve in that office.

How is the president elected? Most Americans assume that the president is elected by popular vote and the candidate with the highest number wins the election. This is not correct and may surprise those who thought they voted for Bill Clinton, Robert Dole, or Ross Perot in 1996. In fact, they voted for Clinton's or Dole's or Perot's electors who then elected the president. In the United States, the voters do not directly select the president. The Constitution provides a fairly complex—and some argue, an outdated—procedure for electing the president. Indeed, the electoral system devised by the Framers and modified by the Twelfth Amendment (1804) is unique. The records of the Constitutional Convention (1787) are silent in explaining the origins of the electoral system, usually referred to as the Electoral College. The several Federalist papers (Nos. 68–71) written by Alexander Hamilton in defense of the electoral system omit any source for the idea.

Under the electoral system of the United States, each state has the number of electoral voters equal to the size of its congressional delegation (House of Representatives plus Senate). Every 10 years, the census, as required by the Constitution, adjusts the number of representatives each state has in the House of Representatives because of population growth or loss. Every state always must have two senators. In the presidential election of 1996, for example, New York State had 33 electoral votes, because New York has 31 representatives and two senators. Alaska had three electoral votes, because Alaska has one representative and two senators. Since every congressional district must be approximately equal in population, we can say that the entire population of Alaska—the largest state in geographic size—is approximately equal in population to the 19th congressional district of New York City which covers the upper part of Manhattan Island.

There are 435 members of the House of Representatives. This number was fixed in 1910. There are 100 members of the Senate (50 states x 2 senators). This equals 535 electors. The Twenty-third Amendment (1961) gives the District of Columbia, the seat of our nation's capital, the electoral vote of the least populous state, three. So, the total electoral vote is 535 plus three or 538. To be elected president, a candidate must receive a majority, that is more than 50 percent, of the electoral votes: 270 electoral votes. If no candidate obtains a majority, the House of Representatives must choose the president from the top three candidates with each state delegation casting one vote. This happened in the 1824 presidential election. (See the article on John Quincy Adams.)

How does a political party choose its presidential nominee? Political parties play a crucial role—they select the candidates and provide the voters with a choice of alternatives.

In the early days of the Republic, the party's membership in Congress—the congressional caucus—chose presidential nominees. Sometimes state and local officials also put forward candidates. National party conventions where delegates were selected by state and local groups began by the 1830s. Each state had different delegate election procedures—some more democratic than others. Custom dictated that the convention sought the candidate. Potential nominees invariably seemed withdrawn and disinterested. They would rarely attend a nominating convention. Any attempt to pursue delegates was considered to be in bad taste. In fact, custom dictated that an official delegation went to the nominee's home to notify him of the party's decision and ask if he would accept. In the early years, convention officials sent a letter. By 1852, the candidate was informed in person. In the 1890s, these notification ceremonies dramatically increased in size. Madison Square Garden in New York City was the site for Grover Cleveland's 1892 notification.

By the first decade of the twentieth century, political reformers considered the convention system most undemocratic. They felt that it was a system dominated by patronage seeking party bosses who ignored the average voter. The primary system began as a way to increase participation in the nominating process. Candidates for the nation's highest office now actually sought the support of convention delegates. Theoretically, the primary allows all party members to choose their party's nominee. Most twentieth century conventions though, have seen a combination of delegates chosen by a political machine and elected in a primary. Today success in the primaries virtually assures the nomination. With few exceptions, the national conventions have become a rubber stamp for the candidate who did the best in the primaries.

The Campaign and Election. The presidential campaign is the great democratic exercise in politics. In recent elections, televised debates between the candidates have become a ritual, attracting record numbers of viewers. Public opinion polls continually monitor the nation's pulse. Commentators and writers analyze campaign strategies. Perhaps the winning strategy is to mobilize the party faithful and to persuade the independent voter that their candidate is the best. This is a costly process and since 1976, the general treasury provides major financial assistance to presidential campaigns. Public funding helps serious presidential candidates to present their qualifications without selling out to wealthy contributors and special interest groups.

Finally, on that first Tuesday after the first Monday in November, the voters make their choice. With the tragic exception of 1860, the American people have accepted the results. (See the article on Abraham Lincoln.) The election process works. Democracy has survived. Forty-one men have held the office of president of the United States. Each has been a powerful personality with varied leadership traits. Each had the opportunity to make major decisions both in foreign and domestic matters which affected the direction of the nation.

Join us as we proceed to study the men who helped to shape our history. We will also learn about their vice presidents, their cabinets, their families, and their homes and monuments.

Fred L. Israel
The City College of the City University of New York

Sir Isaac Newton, the seventeenth-century English scientist who created calculus, discovered that white light is composed of many colors, discovered the law of gravity, and developed the standard laws of motion, once said, "If I have seen farther, it is because I have stood on the shoulders of giants." He meant that he used the work of those who came before him as a starting point for the development of his own ideas. This concept is as true in reference books as it is in science.

The White House Historical Association (740 Jackson Place N.W., Washington, D.C. 20503) supplied all the full page color paintings of the presidents, except seven. They are used with the permission of the White House

Historical Association, and we are grateful to them for their cooperation. The painting of James Monroe is Courtesy of the James Monroe Museum and Memorial Library, Fredericksburg, Virginia; the William Henry Harrison portrait is Courtesy of Grouseland; the John Tyler painting is Courtesy of Sherwood Forest Plantation; the Benjamin Harrison painting is from the President Benjamin Harrison Home; Harry Truman's photograph is from the U.S. Navy, Courtesy Harry S. Truman Library; George Bush's photograph is Courtesy of the Bush Presidential Materials Project; Bill Clinton's photograph is Courtesy of The White House. All the busts of the vice presidents are Courtesy of the Architect of the Capitol.

Over three dozen illustrations are credited to the Collection of David J. and Janice L. Frent. The Frents are friends and neighbors. Fred Israel and I both want to thank them very much for allowing us to show some of the treasures of their unequaled collection of political memorabilia.

The authors of the biographical pieces on the presidents are listed in each volume. They have provided the core of this work, and I am very grateful to them for their cooperation. Dr. Donald A. Ritchie, Associate Historian, United States Senate, wrote all the biographies of the vice presidents. Few people know more about this subject than Dr. Ritchie, and we appreciate his assistance.

Maribeth A. Corona (Editor, Charles E. Smith Books, Inc.) and I have written the sections on Family, Cabinet, and Places. Dr. Israel's editing of our work corrected and improved it greatly although we take full responsibility for any errors that remain. In preparing the material on places, three books served as a starting point: *Presidential Libraries and Museums, An Illustrated Guide,* Pat Hyland (Congressional Quarterly Inc., 1995); *Historic Homes of the American Presidents,* second edition, Irvin Haas (Dover Publications, 1991); and *Cabins, Cottages & Mansions, Homes of the Presidents of the United States,* Nancy D. Myers Benbow and Christopher H. Benbow (Thomas Publications, 1993). We wrote to every place noted in this work and our copy is based on the wealth of information returned to us. It is the most comprehensive and up-to-date collection of information available on this subject.

There is no single book on the families of the presidents. We relied on the abundance of biographies and autobiographies of members of the first families. Also helpful was *Children in the White House,* Christine Sadler (G.P. Putnam's Sons, 1967); *The Presidents' Mothers,* Doris Faber (St. Martin's Press, 1978); and *The First Ladies,* Margaret Brown Klapthor (White House Historical Association, 1989).

The Complete Book of U.S. Presidents, William A. DeGregorio (Wings Books, 1993) is an outstanding one-volume reference work, and we referred to it often. I also had the great pleasure of referring often to three encyclopedias which I had published earlier: *Encyclopedia of the American Presidency,* Leonard W. Levy and Louis Fisher (Simon & Schuster, 1994); *Encyclopedia of the American Constitution,* Leonard W. Levy, Kenneth L. Karst, and Dennis Mahoney (Macmillan & Free Press, 1986); and *Encyclopedia of the United States Congress,* Donald C. Bacon, Roger Davidson, and Morton H. Keller (Simon & Schuster, 1995). I also referred often to *Running for President, The Candidates and Their Images,* Arthur M. Schlesinger, Jr. (Simon & Schuster, 1994). Publishing this two-volume set also gave me the pleasure of working with Professor Schlesinger and the Associate Editors, Fred L. Israel and David J. Frent.

Most of the copyediting was done by Jerilyn Famighetti who was, as usual, prompt, accurate, and pleasant. Our partner in this endeavor was M.E. Aslett Corporation, 95 Campus Plaza, Edison, New Jersey. Although everyone at Aslett lent a hand, special thanks go to Elizabeth Geary, who designed the books; Brian Hewitt and Bob Bovasso, who scanned the images; and Joanne Morbit, who composed the pages. They designed every page and prepared the film for printing. The index was prepared by Jacqueline Flamm.

Charles E. Smith
Freehold, New Jersey

Theodore Roosevelt

CHRONOLOGICAL EVENTS

27 October 1858	Born, New York, New York
30 June 1880	Graduated from Harvard College, Massachusetts
9 November 1881	Elected to New York State Assembly
June 1884	Moved to Medora, Dakota Territory
October 1886	Returned to the East
November 1886	Ran unsuccessfully for mayor of New York
1889	Appointed to U.S. Civil Service Commission
May 1895	Elected president of New York Police Board
5 April 1897	Appointed assistant secretary of the navy
6 May 1898	Resigned as assistant secretary of the navy
5 June 1898	Promoted to colonel of the First U.S. Volunteer Cavalry Regiment, popularly known as the Rough Riders in Spanish-American War
8 November 1898	Elected governor of New York
6 November 1900	Elected vice president
14 September 1901	Became president upon the death of William McKinley
23 February 1904	Hay-Bunau-Varilla Treaty signed; leased Panama canal zone to the United States
8 November 1904	Elected president
6 December 1904	Announced Roosevelt Corollary to the Monroe Doctrine
4 March 1905	Inaugurated president
August 1905	Mediated Russo-Japanese Peace
5 September 1905	Treaty of Portsmouth signed; ended Russo-Japanese War
30 June 1906	Signed Meat Inspection Act and Pure Food and Drug Act
10 December 1906	Awarded Nobel Peace Prize for Treaty of Portsmouth
16 December 1907	Dispatched U.S. Fleet on world cruise
23 March 1909	Departed on 10-month expedition to Africa with his son, Kermit
August 1912	Formed the Progressive (Bull Moose) Party
5 November 1912	Defeated for election as president
1913	Published memoirs, *Theodore Roosevelt: An Autobiography*
August 1914	Outbreak of World War I
April 1917	Request to raise a volunteer division in the event the United States entered the war was denied
6 January 1919	Died, Oyster Bay, New York

BIOGRAPHY

EARLY LIFE. Theodore Roosevelt, the second of four children born to Theodore and Martha Bulloch Roosevelt, was born in New York on 27 October 1858. Although his family was wealthy (his father was a successful banker and merchant), young Theodore's life was a challenging one because of health problems. Frail and troubled by poor vision and asthma, he undertook a rigid and vigorous exercise program that restored his health. His love of the outdoor life is clearly evident through his early interests, which included boxing, hunting, and horseback riding. He was also an avid student of natural history and military affairs.

Roosevelt was educated by private tutors until he entered Harvard College. Soon after graduating from Harvard Phi Beta Kappa in 1880, he married Alice Hathaway Lee. Two years later he published his first major book, *The Naval War of 1812*. At age 23, he was elected to the New York State Assembly, where he championed the regulation of tenement sweatshops. This period of Roosevelt's life, a happy and productive one, came to a sudden end in 1884 when his mother, only 48 years old, died unexpectedly. Less than 12 hours later, and in the very same house, his 22-year-old wife also passed away soon after giving birth to their first child, a girl they named Alice. The date was 14 February, Valentine's Day, and it was the couple's fourth wedding anniversary. Roosevelt, devastated by the twin loss, would note in his diary: "The light has gone out of my life."

The next two years were lonely ones for Roosevelt. He became a cattle rancher in the

Theodore Roosevelt first went to the North Dakota Badlands in 1883 to hunt bison. He had this home, known as the Maltese Cross Cabin, built. He lived as a working cowboy, and he finished writing Hunting Trips of a Ranchman *by lamplight in this cabin. When he returned to the Dakotas in 1884, he started a second ranch, The Elkhorn, about 35 miles away from the Maltese Cross Ranch. Reflecting on the influences that shaped his life, Roosevelt once said, "I never would have been President if it had not been for my experiences in North Dakota."* (Courtesy National Park Service, Theodore Roosevelt National Park; photographer: Thomas C. Gray.)

Dakota Territory while continuing to write history. He published another well-received book, *The Winning of the West*. It is during this period that he cultivated his love for the outdoors while also developing a lasting interest in conservation.

Roosevelt returned to the East in 1886, where he attempted to reenter politics. Success, however, was slow, and Roosevelt finished third in a run for mayor of New York that year. Also in 1886, he married his childhood sweetheart Edith Kermit Carow, who would eventually bear him four sons: Theodore Jr., Kermit, Archibald, and Quentin, and one daughter, Ethel. For the next three years, he lived a life of relative seclusion at his family estate, Sagamore Hill, at Oyster Bay on Long Island, while writing several books on a variety of subjects.

Roosevelt entered public service in 1889, when President Benjamin Harrison appointed him to head the U.S. Civil Service Commission. During his time in this office, he battled against the spoils system, by which politicians rewarded those who had voted for them with jobs and other favors. Roosevelt believed the spoils system to be "a source of corruption" that kept "decent" people out of politics. He also increased the number of jobs to be filled by civil service examinations. Roosevelt continued this spirit of reform as president of the New York Police Board (1895–1897), where he improved morale by initiating a system of promotion based on merit rather than political connections.

Roosevelt entered the national spotlight in 1897, when President William McKinley appointed him assistant secretary of the navy. Roosevelt became a strong advocate of U.S. involvement in Cuba, which had been struggling to free itself from Spanish colonial rule. Convinced that it was the duty of "superior" nations to lead and dominate "inferior" ones, Roosevelt believed that it was in the interest of civilization that English-speaking races be dominant in South Africa and the Western Hemisphere and that every expansion of a great civilized power means a victory for law, order, and righteousness. When war broke out between the United States and Spain in 1898, Roosevelt resigned from the Navy Department and became second in command of the so-called Rough Riders, part of the 17,000 U.S. troops that were preparing to invade Cuba. His subsequent and perhaps reckless charge up Kettle Hill during the Battle of San Juan (Roosevelt had earlier claimed that he was there to get "in on the fun.") established his reputation throughout the United States as a hero. When Roosevelt returned home, Thomas Platt, the Republican leader of New York State, asked him to run for governor.

Despite his new-found status as a national war hero, Roosevelt won the election by fewer than 20,000 votes. As governor of New York, he established policies that earned him vast popular support while antagonizing large corporations and the Republican political machine they controlled. Not only did he impose a tax on corporations, but he also increased teachers' salaries and attempted to improve housing conditions throughout the state. With the death of Vice President Garret Hobart in 1899, New York's business community, furious with Roosevelt's policies, plotted to promote him to the vice presidency. This position was considered a graveyard for ambitious politicians. President McKinley accepted Roosevelt as his running mate, and he was elected vice president of the United States in the Republican landslide of 1900. Tragically, six months into McKinley's second term as president, he was assassinated by Leon Czolgosz, an anarchist in Buffalo, New York. On 14 September 1901, Roosevelt was sworn in as president of the United States. At age 42, he was the youngest ever to hold that office.

PRESIDENCY. As president, Roosevelt brought a level of energy into the White House that was in stark contrast to his predecessors. He played a vigorous game of tennis. He once galloped 100 miles on horseback in a single day. He even boxed with professional opponents, one of whom blinded him in his left eye during one of their matches.

Roosevelt brought the same enthusiasm to the presidency that he brought to his activities outside

On 5 May 1898, Roosevelt resigned his position as assistant secretary of the navy. He served with the First U.S. Volunteer Cavalry Regiment, popularly known as the Rough Riders, from May to September 1898. When the commander of the regiment, Leonard Wood, was promoted, Roosevelt became the colonel of the regiment.

Roosevelt led the attack at Kettle Hill in Cuba, which became known as the charge up San Juan Hill. It made him a national hero. Just a little more than three years later, he was the youngest president in history.

(Harper's Pictorial History of the War with Spain, Courtesy Collection of Charles E. Smith.)

the presidency. Although he had publicly pledged to continue the conservative policies of McKinley, he soon moved far beyond them. Despite surrounding himself with such capable advisers as John Hay in the State Department and Elihu Root in the Department of War, Roosevelt believed that the president should be the main shaper of legislative policy. The rest of his term in office offered ample evidence of his belief in a strong and independent chief executive.

In this regard, Roosevelt considered himself the leader of "all" American people, not just business executives, and his emergence as a national leader coincides with what historians have since labeled the Progressive Era in U.S. history. The United States by this time had settled the continent from coast to coast and had carved out the beginnings of an industrial empire. Roosevelt felt that farmers, small business owners, and laborers were as deserving of the protection of the law as were large corporations. For the next seven and one-half years, he fought to manage society in such a way that the nation could develop in a peaceful and orderly manner. The nation had been hit with a devastating depression in the 1890s, and the hard times that this had brought to the cities had alarmed many members of the growing middle and upper middle class who had prospered from the country's rapid industrialization.

It was an age of increasing social awareness as well as growing idealism, aided in no small part by a group of journalists known collectively as "muckrakers." They were given this name by Roosevelt himself, who compared them to a character in John Bunyan's *Pilgrim's Progress* who constantly spread dirt, or muck, on the floor below him, so much so that he was prevented from seeing all the good things in life that were happening all around him. It was not an entirely complimentary term; Roosevelt felt that these writers were adding to the discontent felt by many of the urban poor, but he recognized that their intent was to get people angry enough to fight against social wrong. Ida Tarbell illustrated the cutthroat methods corporations used to eliminate competition in her *History of the Standard Oil Company*. In *The Shame of the Cities*, Lincoln Steffens exposed the corrupt influence of big business on crooked politicians, and in 1906, Upton Sinclair, in *The Jungle*, shocked the entire nation by writing in detail of the filthy conditions of the meat-packing industry in Chicago.

To increase national unity, Roosevelt initiated programs that he referred to as "the square deal," so named because, through the expansion of Roosevelt's powers, the average person would benefit "squarely." In his first annual message to the nation, delivered in December 1901, Roosevelt endorsed the "sincere conviction that [corporate] combination and concentration should be, not prohibited, but supervised and within reasonable limits controlled." The twin pillars of his "square deal" would be stricter control of big business and stronger enforcement of the antitrust laws that were already in effect.

What Roosevelt sought, despite his reputation as a trustbuster, was a combination of business firms formed by a legal agreement with the intention of reducing competition. He merely wanted to control them. There is thus a cautious note of conservatism in his policies. He desired a middle ground between the laissez-faire individualism (government noninterference in the affairs of big business) that had previously been the accepted way of things and the extremes of socialist philosophy (advocating a state-run economy) that were beginning to be heard throughout the nation. He initiated antitrust proceedings against the Northern Securities Company, a huge railroad trust created by some of the nation's richest and most powerful businessmen, among them John D. Rockefeller, Edward Harriman, and J. P. Morgan. Roosevelt also mediated a Pennsylvania coal strike in 1902, in which the issues were labor's right to organize into a union, its demand for an eight-hour day, and higher wages. When Roosevelt threatened to seize the mines and have the army run them, the mine operators eventually agreed to the demands of an eight-hour day and a 10 percent pay increase.

President Roosevelt made three appointments to the Supreme Court: Oliver Wendell Holmes, William R. Day, and William H. Moody.

Holmes (shown here) served as associate justice from 1902 to 1932. He is perhaps the most highly regarded associate justice in the history of the Supreme Court. Roosevelt expected him to be a consistent supporter of his own progressive ideals and was bitterly disappointed when he proved not to be so. (Courtesy Library of Congress).

FIRST ANNUAL MESSAGE TO CONGRESS

. . . There is a widespread conviction in the minds of the American people that the great corporations known as trusts are in certain of their features and tendencies hurtful to the general welfare. This . . . based upon sincere conviction that combination and concentration should be, not prohibited, but supervised and within reasonable limits controlled; and in my judgment this conviction is right.

It is no limitation upon property rights or freedom of contract to require that when men receive from government the privilege of doing business under corporate form, which frees them from individual responsibility, and enables them to call into their enterprises the capital of the public, they shall do so upon absolutely truthful representations as to the value of the property in which the capital is to be invested. Corporations engaged in interstate commerce should be regulated if they are found to exercise a license working to the public injury. It should be as much the aim of those who seek for social betterment to rid the business world of crimes of cunning as to rid the entire body politic of crimes of violence. Great corporations exist only because they are created and safeguarded by our institutions; and it is therefore our right and our duty to see that they work in harmony with these institutions. . . .

• *President Roosevelt delivered this message to Congress on 3 December 1901. Although he was known as a trustbuster, this message shows that what he sought was control over the trusts, not their elimination.*

However, the miners failed to obtain a closed shop for the mine (an agreement by which management consents to hire only union members) and agreed not to strike again for at least three years. Of particular importance in this strike is the fact that Roosevelt, through his threat of sending in federal troops to control the mines, was in effect saying that the federal government had not only the right but also the duty to intervene in a strike if the public welfare was threatened. It is not surprising, then, to learn of the comments of the Detroit *Free Press* concerning his actions in the Northern Securities Case, which noted that "Wall Street is paralyzed at the thought that a President . . . would sink so low as to try to enforce the law."

Throughout his term Roosevelt echoed the Progressive belief that problems could and should be solved in an orderly way, and many of his efforts centered on filing suits under the much-neglected Sherman Antitrust Act (1890). Among his targets were the beef trust, the sugar trust, the steel trust, and the oil trust. In fact, during his presidency, the government initiated 44 different antitrust suits. (Roosevelt, however, continued to claim that it was not corporate bigness that he opposed, but wrongdoing.) He never tired in his efforts to secure a more ordered and a more efficient society. In one year alone, 1906, he was able to sign three significant pieces of legislation, the Hepburn Railway Rate Act, which enabled the Interstate Commerce Commission to establish railroad rates; the Pure Food and Drug Act; and a measure that required inspection of all meat-packing plants. Often, he signed these laws in the face of stiff congressional opposition. Many members of Congress were still influenced by business leaders convinced that Roosevelt was out to destroy them.

CONSERVATION. In another sphere, Roosevelt initiated a host of conservation policies, in an acknowledgment that the country's natural resources were being exploited for private profit. The days when the United States was a land of clear

The Conservation of Natural Resources

. . . The conservation of our natural resources and their proper use constitute the fundamental problem which underlies almost every other problem of our national life. . . . As a nation we not only enjoy a wonderful measure of present prosperity but if this prosperity is used aright it is an earnest of future success such as no other nation will have. The reward of foresight for this nation is great and easily foretold. But there must be the look ahead, there must be a realization of the fact that to waste, to destroy, our natural resources, to skin and exhaust the land instead of using it so as to increase its usefulness, will result in undermining in the days of our children the very prosperity which we ought by right to hand down to them amplified and developed. For the last few years, through several agencies, the government has been endeavoring to get our people to look ahead and to substitute a planned and orderly development of our resources in place of a haphazard striving for immediate profit. . . .

- *President Roosevelt delivered these remarks in his Seventh Annual Message to Congress on 3 December 1907. His record in dealing with environmental issues remains unmatched.*

rivers and untamed forests were long over. Now, municipalities often drained dirty water and industrial waste into the rivers, creating unseen health hazards for their residents. As ranchers allowed their livestock to overgraze the Great Plains, the prairies of the nation's heartland were no longer able to sustain the animal population that depended on them. Huge industrial concerns spewed toxic waste into the air. Lumber companies proved constantly that the Forest Bureau, which had been created in 1887, was nothing more than a pretense by completely ignoring its rulings and advisories.

In dealing with these problems, Roosevelt acted with characteristic decisiveness and enthusiasm. His record in dealing with environmental issues is still unmatched. In 1903, he signed into law the Newlands Act, under which 30 irrigation projects were either begun or completed while he was in office. Two years later, he reorganized the Forest Service and placed it under the capable and determined leadership of Gifford Pinchot. In effect, he signaled to lumber companies that they would henceforth have to obey all the rules of national law. He increased the total area of national forests from 43 to 194 million acres and doubled the number of national parks. He established 16 national monuments and 51 wildlife preserves. Years later, with the completion of the Roosevelt Dam in Arizona as part of the long-term payoff of the Reclamation Act of June 1902, a vast desert would be transformed into a fertile and productive farming region. In March 1907, he established the Inland Waterways Commission. Fourteen months later, he presided over a national conference of state governors called to consider only issues that related to the environment. All these actions added to the public perception that, unlike in previous generations, government now acted on behalf of all the people of the United States. This new-found reliance in the positive power of government partly explains Roosevelt's victory over Alton B. Parker in the presidential election of 1904. Roosevelt won by more than 2.5 million votes. That was the largest majority ever received by a presidential candidate up to that time.

FOREIGN POLICY. Roosevelt had an equally lasting effect on the foreign policy of the United States, which he conducted with both prudence and real-

Theodore Roosevelt placed his conservation of natural resources second only to the beginning of the Panama Canal among his achievements as president. He said, in his first message to Congress, that water and forest problems were the most important matters facing the country. Roosevelt spoke at the dedication ceremonies of Roosevelt Dam, Arizona. (Courtesy National Archives.)

ism. While willing to invoke force in pursuit of the national interest, he believed in the virtue of preparedness as a means of preventing war. During his presidency, he greatly increased the strength and efficiency of the army and the navy.

In the wake of the Spanish-American War, the United States was becoming increasingly involved with the countries in the Caribbean Sea. The one dominant issue was the possible construction of a canal through the isthmus of Panama, at that time a province of Colombia. While the United States had long dreamed of building an interoceanic canal there as a stimulant to international trade, several factors complicated the project. A French company had already begun work on a canal. From 1881 to 1887, it had invested some $300 million. More than 20,000 workers had died while working on the project. Although less than a third of the canal was completed, this company owned the rights to the canal and would have to be paid, and paid handsomely, to forfeit its claim. Further complicating things was Panama itself, which sought $10 million from the United States for the right to build the canal, and then suddenly increased its demand to $25 million.

To sidestep these problems, Roosevelt, with the advice of Secretary of State Hay, decided to offer covert assistance to a group of Panamanian rebels by having a U.S. battleship obstruct the efforts of the Colombian army to suppress their revolt. The United States would then negotiate with the successful revolutionaries for the rights to build a canal at a price more acceptable to the United States. While Colombia did eventually receive $25 million from the administration of Warren G. Harding, Roosevelt's boast that "I stole Panama" is now considered one of the biggest blunders ever in U.S. foreign policy. It needlessly offended the countries of Latin America at a time when the United States should have been attempting to cultivate friendships with them. The incident changed their view of their powerful neighbor to the north as an arrogant bully. Although the canal did prove to benefit both the Panamanian and the U.S. economies after its opening on 15 August 1914 (less than two weeks after the start of World War I), U.S. ownership of the canal remained a delicate issue between the two countries. Finally, in 1978, President Jimmy Carter agreed to cede control of it to Panama in 1998.

Roosevelt had other concerns in the area besides the canal. When countries in the Caribbean region fell behind in the payment of their foreign debt, several European military powers threatened them with intervention. Since the Monroe Doctrine was issued in 1823, U.S. policy had been to oppose European attempts at colonization in any part of the Western Hemisphere. In 1904, as a result of a crisis over the debt accumulated by the Dominican Republic, Roosevelt issued what came to be known as the Roosevelt Corollary to the Monroe Doctrine. Roosevelt stated that the United States was justified in intervening in the region to prevent other nations from taking action there. In essence, Roosevelt suggested that the United States could exercise an "international police power" within the region. While his stand was successful in bringing about a peaceful settlement to the Dominican debt crisis in 1905, it served as the basis for a far more active involvement in the region in later years.

Roosevelt did not confine his international diplomacy to the Caribbean. Although one of the first U.S. politicians to recognize the commercial appeal of the Far East as well as its eventual importance in world politics, he abandoned the notion, popular among many European powers at the time, that a strong nation needed a widespread empire to define its greatness. Consistent with his actions in the Caribbean, he once again combined the daring of a military man with the tact of a politician in dealing with issues in Asia. He won international prestige for his actions in bringing about an end to the Russo-Japanese War in 1905, and a year later was awarded the Nobel Peace Prize in recognition of these efforts. In 1907, he concluded his famous Gentleman's Agreement in which he forced the San Francisco school board to repeal its policy of segregating Japanese schoolchildren in return for a Japanese curb on emigration of poor people and

The Roosevelt Corollary to the Monroe Doctrine

. . . It is not true that the United States feels any land hunger or entertains any projects as regards the other nations of the Western Hemisphere save such as are for their welfare. All that this country desires is to see the neighboring countries stable, orderly, and prosperous. Any country whose people conduct themselves well can count upon our hearty friendship. If a nation shows that it knows how to act with reasonable efficiency and decency in social and political matters, if it keeps order and pays its obligations, it need fear no interference from the United States. Chronic wrongdoing, or an impotence which results in a general loosening of the ties of civilized society, may in America, as elsewhere, ultimately require intervention by some civilized nation, and in the Western Hemisphere the adherence of the United States to the Monroe Doctrine may force the United States, however reluctantly, in flagrant cases of such wrongdoing or impotence, to the exercise of an international police power. If every country washed by the Caribbean Sea would show the progress in stable and just civilization which with the aid of the Platt amendment Cuba has shown since our troops left the island, and which so many of the republics in both Americas are constantly and brilliantly showing, all question of interference by this Nation with their affairs would be at an end. Our interests and those of our southern neighbors are in reality identical. They have great natural riches, and if within their borders the reign of law and justice obtains, prosperity is sure to come to them. While they thus obey the primary laws of civilized society they may rest assured that they will be treated by us in a spirit of cordial and helpful sympathy. We would interfere with them only in the last resort, and then only if it became evident that their inability or unwillingness to do justice at home and abroad had violated the rights of the United States or had invited foreign aggression to the detriment of the entire body of American nations. It is a mere truism to say that every nation, whether in America or anywhere else, which desires to maintain its freedom, its independence, must ultimately realize that the right of such independence can not be separated from the responsibility of making good use of it.

In asserting the Monroe Doctrine, in taking such steps as we have taken in regard to Cuba, Venezuela, and Panama, and in endeavoring to circumscribe the theater of war in the Far East, and to secure the open door in China, we have acted in our own interest as well as in the interest of humanity at large. There are, however, cases in which, while our own interests are not greatly involved, strong appeal is made to our sympathies. . . . But in extreme cases action may be justifiable and proper. What form the action shall take must depend upon the circumstances of the case; that is, upon the degree of the atrocity and upon our power to remedy it. The cases in which we could interfere by force of arms as we interfered to put a stop to intolerable conditions in Cuba are necessarily very few.

- *President Roosevelt spelled out what came to be known as the Roosevelt Corollary to the Monroe Doctrine in his annual messages to Congress in 1904 and 1905. It was a policy that allowed the United States to take action in any part of the Western Hemisphere in order to prevent other nations from doing so. He claimed that such action was justified by the Monroe Doctrine.*

President Roosevelt was the first American to be awarded the Nobel Peace Prize. He negotiated an end to the Russo-Japanese War, and a peace treaty was signed in Portsmouth, New Hampshire in September 1905. Roosevelt later donated the prize money, grown to almost $50,000, to war victims after the United States entered World War I.

This cotton banner shows a Rough Riders scene at the top. The two men seated are Serge Witte (left), Russia, and Jutaro Komura, Japan. (Courtesy Collection of David J. and Janice L. Frent.)

laborers heading to the United States. He urged that Japan be included among the "superior" nations that seemed destined to dominate world affairs. He also supported the creation of the international court of arbitration at The Hague in the Netherlands. In 1905, two years after claiming that "I fail to understand how any man...could be anything but an expansionist," he forced the Chinese government, against its will, to end its boycott of U.S. goods. Two years later, taking a "big stick" approach to international diplomacy, he sailed the "Great White Fleet" of the U.S. navy around the world to display the nation's military power.

POST PRESIDENTIAL YEARS. The Great White Fleet returned to the United States in February 1909, ending Roosevelt's presidency on a rousing note. He had decided in 1904 not to run for a second full term as president and handpicked Secretary of War William Howard Taft to be his successor. After Taft's inauguration in March 1909, Roosevelt took an extended trip to Africa to hunt and collect fauna, returning home in 1910 to a warm and enthusiastic welcome.

A quiet retirement did not await him. Taft had deserted the Progressive reforms of his predecessor, and this caused the Republicans to suffer many setbacks in the congressional elections of 1910. As public disenchantment with Taft grew, Roosevelt's followers urged him to reenter the political arena. In August of 1910, in Kansas, Roosevelt delivered one of the most important speeches of his political career, which he cleverly titled the "New Nationalism." In it, he defined the political agenda that would identify him for the rest of his public political life. He moved far beyond the Progressive achievements of his presidency, issuing a call for new federal reforms, including the initiative (the proposal of legislation for popular vote by voters' petition), the recall (the removal from office of an official by popular vote), and the referendum (the right of the people to vote on proposed laws). Roosevelt would later claim that he was trying to save his country from revolution: "What I have advocated is not wild radicalism. It is the highest and wisest kind of conservatism."

. . . Constitution-makers should make it clear beyond shadow of doubt that the people in their legislative capacity have the power to enact into law any measure they deem necessary for the betterment of social and industrial conditions. The wisdom of framing any particular law of this kind is a proper subject of debate; but the power of the people to enact the law should not be subject to debate. To hold the contrary view is to be false to the cause of the people, to the cause of American democracy. . . .

We stand for the rights of property, but we stand even more for the rights of man.

We will protect the rights of the wealthy man, but we maintain that he holds his wealth subject to the general right of the community to regulate its business use as the public welfare requires. . . .

• *Excerpt from Theodore Roosevelt's speech, New Nationalism, a recurring theme. He delivered this speech on 21 February 1912 at the Ohio Constitutional Convention in Columbus, Ohio.*

Sensing the political weaknesses of Taft, his former secretary of war, Roosevelt officially entered the presidential race in February 1912. Although victorious in most of the political primaries that year, even in Taft's home state of Ohio, Roosevelt was still not able to take the Republican nomination from Taft, who was able to use his advantage as president and party leader to preserve the nomination for himself. Amid accusations of political backstabbing and claiming that he felt "fit as a bull moose," Roosevelt went on to run as a third-party candidate that year, heading a political coalition that was named for his description of his physical health. But the division within the Republican Party could not be overcome, and in 1912 the Democratic candidate Woodrow Wilson, a moderately progressive governor from New Jersey, overwhelmingly

Roosevelt was chosen as the presidential candidate of the Progressive (Bull Moose) Party at its convention in August 1912 in Chicago. He campaigned by criss-crossing the country by train, making three or four major speeches a day. (Courtesy National Archives.)

won the election, receiving 435 electoral votes and 6,293,097 popular votes to Roosevelt's 88 electoral votes and 4,119,507 popular votes. Taft, the incumbent president, won only 8 electoral votes and 3,438,956 popular votes, while Eugene Debs, a Socialist, received 901,873 popular votes in the election. The election was noted for an attempt on Roosevelt's life at a campaign stop in Milwaukee, Wisconsin on 14 October. The wounded former president still insisted on speaking to the crowd.

In the two years after Wilson's election, Roosevelt lived a life of comparative peace and quiet, writing his autobiography and, at the suggestion of the Brazilian government, leading an expedition up an uncharted river in that country. On the trip, Roosevelt grew desperately ill and nearly died of malarial fever. In 1914, still loyal to the Progressive cause, he campaigned unsuccessfully for many Progressive Party candidates in the congressional elections.

When war broke out in Europe, Roosevelt immediately rallied to the cause of U.S. preparation for possible involvement in the hostilities. He campaigned actively in 1915 for U.S. entry into the war on the side of the Allies, while warning of the implications of a German victory and control of the European landmass. During these years, he grew increasingly frustrated at the "peace at any price" policies of Wilson and sought to defeat him in his bid for reelection in 1916. However, satisfied that the Republican presidential nominee, U.S. Supreme Court Justice Charles Evans Hughes, offered a solid alternative to U.S. voters, he refused the Bull Moose nomination to run for president one more time.

The sinking of the British ocean liner *Lusitania* on 7 May 1915 resulted in the loss of 128 U.S. lives. Roosevelt grew more and more impatient at what he perceived to be the "timid and inept" leadership of Wilson. With the official U.S. entry into the war on Good Friday 1917, he sought but was refused an active military commission. He found consolation in immersing himself in the military activities of his four sons, and in campaigning actively for the Liberty Loan Program, the Red Cross, and other relief agencies. As proof of his enduring appeal to the U.S. public, more than a quarter million men volunteered to serve under him when the United States officially entered the war. Tragedy, though, continued to haunt Roosevelt. After his youngest son, Quentin, died in the war, Roosevelt wrote that "only those are fit to live who do not fear to die, and none are fit to die who have shrunk from the joy of life and the duty of life. Both life and death are part of the same Great Adventure."

For Roosevelt, his own Great Adventure was coming to a close. With the end of the war in 1918, the former president ridiculed Wilson's Fourteen Points as "Fourteen Scraps of Paper" and called for the continued preservation of the Monroe Doctrine, as well as for U.S. entry into the League of Nations. But for the man who had once proclaimed himself as "fit as a bull moose," time was rapidly running out. On 6 January 1919, he died quietly in his sleep. "The old lion is dead," his son, Archie, cabled his brothers. He was buried in a simple ceremony at the family estate at Sagamore Hill.

SUMMARY. Theodore Roosevelt was many things. One of the most colorful U.S. presidents, he was also a writer, a soldier, an orator, a naturalist, and an historian. He was, in the words of a friend, "a man who could do so much [who] could not do everything perfectly, though few have ever done so many things as well."

Accused of being egotistic, and at times even ruthless, he was often a controversial president, although, by whatever yardstick one may choose to use, an extraordinarily popular one as well. Not only did he tremendously expand the power of the presidential office, he also increased the role of the United States in world affairs, pushing it to a position of predominance in the Western Hemisphere.

While encouraging the growth of organized labor during his years in the White House, he signaled to corporate America that no corporation was so powerful as to be beyond the reach of the law. As the first president-reformer, he oversaw an increase in government regulation of business and increased the impact of the federal government, often beneficially, in every citizen's life. This is evident in his enduring legacy as a conservationist.

Roosevelt caused all Americans to reexamine their sense of civic responsibility, and, while demanding from them that they take responsibility for being better citizens, he allowed them to demand from government their right to live a life free from corporate abuse or government neglect. He could never escape his upper-class origins, and can be viewed as a "have" looking out for and caring for those who "have not." He was an American original and has come to symbolize all that is good, as well as some that is bad, in the country he loved so much.

"Ironically, Roosevelt's ex-presidency probably made a bigger impact on American politics than his presidency. His leadership of the Progressives and his articulation of the New Nationalism unquestionably reshaped the course of domestic politics. His stands on defense and foreign policy during World War I undoubtedly altered the course of American diplomacy at a critical juncture. Even though he did not achieve these results by occupying the White House, he was able to accomplish more on the outside during the last ten years of his life than most Presidents have accomplished from the inside. The ex-presidency of Theodore Roosevelt completed the legacy of his presidency." John Milton Cooper, Jr., "Roosevelt, Theodore" in Encyclopedia of the American Presidency, *edited by Leonard W. Levy and Louis Fisher.* (Courtesy Library of Congress.)

VICE PRESIDENT

Charles Warren Fairbanks (1852–1918)

CHRONOLOGICAL EVENTS

1852	Born, Unionville Center, Ohio, 11 May
1872	Graduated from Ohio Wesleyan University
1896	Elected to U.S. Senate
1904	Elected vice president
1916	Ran unsuccessfully for vice president
1918	Died, Indianapolis, Indiana, 4 June

BIOGRAPHY

The son of a prosperous farmer and wagon maker, Charles Fairbanks attended Ohio Wesleyan University and the Cleveland Law College. After his marriage, Fairbanks moved to Indianapolis, Indiana to become an attorney for the Chesapeake and Ohio Railroad, whose general manager was his uncle. Fairbanks's railroad law practice made him wealthy, and his prosecution of railroad strikers in 1877 made him well known within Republican political circles. Before running for office himself, Fairbanks gained control of the Republican Party in Indiana. He made campaign contributions to help Republican candidates across the state. He also purchased ownership of the state's major newspapers to support his political activities.

Fairbanks campaigned vigorously on behalf of William McKinley for president in 1896. The Republican sweep of Indiana that year led to his own election as senator. In the U.S. Senate, he loyally supported McKinley. Appointed a member of the commission to decide the Alaskan boundary with Canada, he stood firm against yielding any territory. As a result, the city of Fairbanks, Alaska was named for him.

Although the Progressive movement spread within his party, Fairbanks remained a prominent member of the Republican "Old Guard." He sparred frequently with his progressive colleague from Indiana, Senator Albert J. Beveridge, and never felt as close to President Theodore Roosevelt as he had been to McKinley. Fairbanks had presidential ambitions but could not mount a challenge to Roosevelt's renomination in 1904. To balance the ticket, conservatives nominated Fairbanks for vice president. Roosevelt being ardent and progressive, and Fairbanks being cool and conservative, the two men had little in common. Vice President Fairbanks generally identified with the more conservative Senate against the President.

When Roosevelt declined to run for a third term in 1908, Fairbanks sought to advance to the presidency. But Roosevelt blocked him by recommending Secretary of War William Howard Taft for the Republican presidential nomination. Taft was elected, but Roosevelt found him too conservative as president and ran against him on the Progressive Party ticket in 1912. The split in the Republican Party elected the Democrat Woodrow Wilson president. Advocating party unity, Fairbanks made a last try for the presidential nomination in 1916. Against his wishes, the convention chose him to run for vice president again, this time with New York Governor Charles Evans Hughes. Fairbanks reluctantly agreed because of party loyalty, but the ticket lost narrowly to Wilson. Fairbanks died two years later.

THE CABINET

SECRETARY OF STATE
John M. Hay, 1901, 1905
Elihu Root, 1905
Robert Bacon, 1905

SECRETARY OF WAR
Elihu Root, 1901
William Howard Taft, 1904, 1905
Luke E. Wright, 1908

SECRETARY OF THE TREASURY
Lyman J. Gage, 1901
Leslie M. Shaw, 1902, 1905
George B. Cortelyou, 1907

POSTMASTER GENERAL
Charles Emory Smith, 1901
Henry C. Payne, 1902
Robert J. Wynne, 1904, 1905
George B. Cortelyou, 1905
George von L. Meyer, 1907

ATTORNEY GENERAL
Philander C. Knox, 1901
William H. Moody, 1904, 1905
Charles J. Bonaparte, 1906

SECRETARY OF THE NAVY
John D. Long, 1901
William H. Moody, 1902
Paul Morton, 1904, 1905
Charles J. Bonaparte, 1905
Victor H. Metcalf, 1906
Trueman H. Newberry, 1908

SECRETARY OF THE INTERIOR
Ethan A. Hitchcock, 1901, 1905
James R. Garfield, 1907

SECRETARY OF AGRICULTURE
James Wilson, 1901, 1905

SECRETARY OF COMMERCE AND LABOR[1]
George B. Cortelyou, 1903
Victor H. Metcalf, 1904, 1905
Oscar S. Straus, 1906

1. Department of Commerce and Labor established 14 February 1903; on 4 March 1913 divided into separate departments. The secretary of each was made a cabinet member.

John D. Long is shown here being questioned by reporters about the situation in Cuba, 1898. Drawing by W.A. Rogers. (*Harper's Pictorial History of the War with Spain, Volume I*, Courtesy Collection Charles E. Smith.)

John D. Long (1838–1915). Long was appointed secretary of the navy by President William McKinley in 1897. After the assassination of McKinley, he retained his post in the administration of Theodore Roosevelt.

Theodore Roosevelt had served as Long's assistant secretary of the navy (1897–1898). Long had said of him: "He is full of suggestions, many of which are of great value, and his spirit and forceful habit is a good tonic; but the very devil seems to possess him—distributing ships, ordering ammunition which there is no means to move to places where there is no means to store it; sending messages to Congress for immediate legislation authorizing the enlistment of an unlimited number of seamen."

As secretary of the navy, Long directed all naval operations during the Spanish-American War. After leaving office in 1902, he wrote *The New American Navy.*

John M. Hay is shown here signing the 1899 memorandum of the treaty ratification which officially ended the Spanish-American War. (*Harper's Pictorial History of the War with Spain, Volume II*, Courtesy Collection of Charles E. Smith.)

John M. Hay (1838–1905). Hay was appointed secretary of state by President William McKinley in 1898. He had previously served as assistant private secretary to President Abraham Lincoln (1861–1865) and ambassador to Great Britain (1897–1898). After the assassination of McKinley, he retained his post in the administration of Theodore Roosevelt.

As secretary of state, Hay approved the annexation of the Philippines and pursued an Open Door Policy with China. (Doctrine of the United States asserting its equal commercial and industrial rights in China.) He also concluded the Hay-Pauncefote Treaty (1901) with Great Britain which made it possible for the United States to build the Panama Canal. He died in office.

FAMILY

CHRONOLOGICAL EVENTS

29 July 1861	Alice Hathaway Lee born	13 September 1887	Son, Theodore, born
6 August 1861	Edith Kermit Carow born	10 October 1889	Son, Kermit, born
27 October 1880	Alice Lee married Theodore Roosevelt	13 August 1891	Daughter, Ethel, born
		9 April 1894	Son, Archibald, born
12 February 1884	Daughter, Alice, born	19 November 1897	Son, Quentin, born
14 February 1884	Alice Lee Roosevelt died	6 January 1919	Theodore Roosevelt died
2 December 1886	Edith Kermit Carow married Theodore Roosevelt	30 September 1948	Edith Roosevelt died

(Courtesy Library of Congress.)

Alice Roosevelt was Theodore Roosevelt's only child by his marriage to Alice Lee. Alice's mother died two days after giving birth to her. Alice was 17 years of age when her father became President. She was as outspoken as her father and soon became known as "Princess Alice."

When the President was asked why he could not make her behave, he said that he could be President of the United States, or he could control Alice, but that he could not do both.

Alice made her debut in the White House on New Year's Eve, 1902. In 1906, she married Nicholas Longworth, a member of the U.S. House of Representatives. He became Speaker of the House, and they were a popular and powerful couple.

She remained at the center of Washington society until her death at the age of 97, during the Kennedy administration. Long before then, she had become known as "Washington's other monument."

Theodore Roosevelt and his second wife, Edith Kermit Carow, had four sons and one daughter. They all followed their father's example of service to their country. Theodore, Jr. was injured in a gas attack in World War I and was appointed assistant secretary of the navy by President Warren G. Harding. He was a brigadier general when he landed with the first wave at Normandy on D-Day. He died of a heart attack soon after and was awarded the Medal of Honor. Kermit served with both the British Army and the U.S. Army in World Wars I and II. He died of natural causes while on active duty.

Ethel married Dr. Richard Derby, and they went to France with the American Ambulance Corps during World War I.

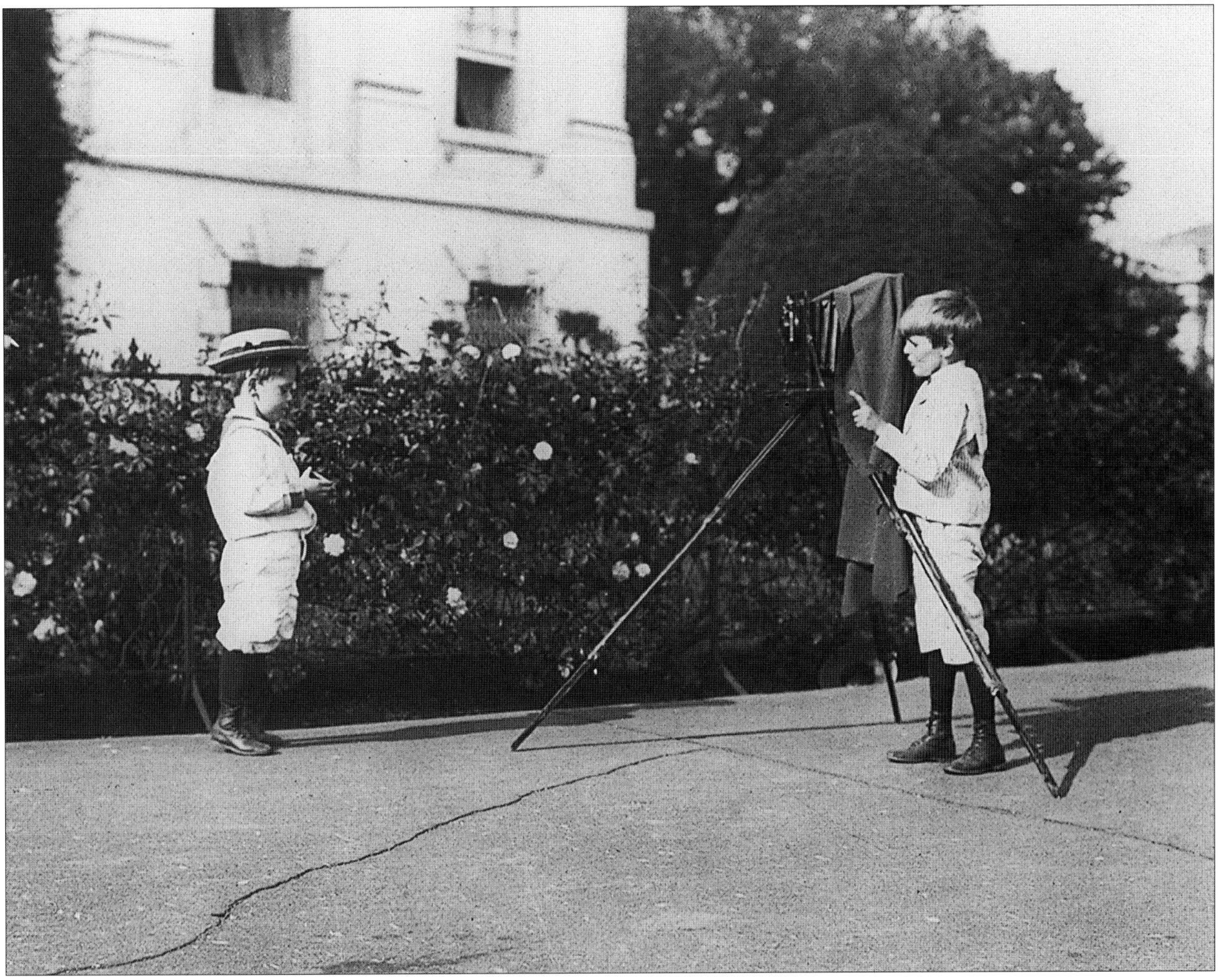

Archie (right) and Quentin are shown here when they were children playing at the White House. Archie graduated from Harvard and was a captain in the army in World War I. He was seriously wounded and discharged as disabled. In World War II, he served in the Pacific as a lieutenant colonel. He was seriously wounded again, and he was again discharged as disabled.

Quentin was a pilot in the Army Air Corps in World War I. He was shot down and killed by German planes, when he was only 20 years old. (Courtesy Library of Congress.)

THEODORE ROOSEVELT BIRTHPLACE NATIONAL HISTORIC SITE

28 East Twentieth Street • New York, New York 10003 • Tel: (212) 260-1616

Located in Manhattan. Can be reached via IRT and BMT subway stops at Twenty-third and Fourteenth streets. Open Wednesday through Saturday from 9 A.M. to 4:30 P.M. Closed Thanksgiving, Christmas, New Year's Day, and all Federal holidays. Admission fee. Senior citizens ages 62 and over, and children ages 16 and under, admitted free. Tours available. Not handicapped accessible. Administered by the National Park Service, U.S. Department of the Interior, in cooperation with the Theodore Roosevelt Association.

In 1854, Theodore Roosevelt's grandfather, Cornelius, purchased the three-story brownstone house as a wedding gift for his son, Theodore, Sr., and his new daughter-in-law, Martha Bulloch. On 27 October 1858, Theodore, Jr.—the future president—was born in the front bedroom of the home. In 1865, Theodore's parents had Leon Marcotte, a leading New York interior decorator, renovate the birthplace home. A fourth floor was added at that time. TR lived there until the fall of 1872, when he and his family set out on a one-year tour of Europe. On their return, they moved into their new home at 6 West Fifty-seventh Street.

The birthplace home remained in the Roosevelt family until 1896, when it was sold and then renovated for a business. Twenty years later, the site was purchased by a developer who demolished it to make way for a small commercial building. After Roosevelt's death in 1919, the Women's Roosevelt Memorial Association was formed, and plans were made for the birthplace reconstruction. Museum galleries and other facilities were built on the adjoining lot where the home of Robert Roosevelt, Theodore's uncle, once stood. The site was opened to the public on 27 October 1923, the 65th anniversary of Roosevelt's birth. In 1963, the Theodore Roosevelt Association donated the site to the National Park Service.

The reconstructed birthplace home has been restored to the period of Roosevelt's boyhood (1865-1872). Approximately 40 percent of the furnishings came from the original home. (Courtesy Eastern National Park & Monument Association.)

◀ *Theodore Roosevelt, Jr. was born in the front bedroom of the Twentieth Street, New York, home in 1858. Today, the room is furnished with original 1866 furniture. A portrait of his mother hangs over the mantel.* (Courtesy Eastern National Park & Monument Association.)

SAGAMORE HILL NATIONAL HISTORIC SITE

20 Sagamore Hill Road • Oyster Bay, New York 11771-1899 • Tel: (516) 922-4788

Located in Cove Neck, Long Island. Can be reached via the Long Island Expressway to Exit 41 North to NY 106 North. This leads directly to Oyster Bay; follow signs. Open daily from 9:30 A.M. to 5 P.M. Closed Thanksgiving, Christmas, and New Year's Day. Admission fee. Senior citizens ages 62 and over, and children ages 15 and under admitted free. Call site prior to visit for current visitation policies. A taped tour, narrated by Theodore Roosevelt's daughter, Ethel, is available for a small fee. Handicapped accessible. The site contains the house and grounds, the Old Orchard Museum, a garden, a pet cemetery, and a gift shop. Administered by the National Park Service, U.S. Department of the Interior.

In March 1884, following the death of his first wife, Alice, Theodore Roosevelt—determined to provide a suitable home for his newborn daughter—signed a contract for the construction of Sagamore Hill, a 22-room Victorian home with 10 fireplaces. In 1885, he moved in with his sister, Anna, and his newborn daughter. He married Edith Carow in December 1886 and lived there until his death in 1919.

After Roosevelt's death, his widow continued to live at Sagamore Hill. Shortly after her death in 1948, the Theodore Roosevelt Association purchased Sagamore Hill, its contents, and 83 acres of surrounding land. In June 1953, it was opened to the public at a dedication ceremony conducted by President Eisenhower. Ten years later, the association donated the site to the American people, and it is now administered by the National Park Service. In 1966, Old Orchard, the home of Roosevelt's son, Theodore, Jr., was opened to the public as the Old Orchard Museum.

During Theodore Roosevelt's presidency, Sagamore Hill became the Summer White House. Many domestic and foreign policy conferences were held there. The home was named for Sagamore Mohannis, the American Indian leader who had lived on the land two centuries earlier. (Courtesy Library of Congress.) ▶

themselves to stabilize the islands. In 1900, he asked Taft to become commissioner of the Philippine government, confident that his fairness and ability would make him successful. Taft took the position without enthusiasm (after McKinley promised to appoint him to the next Supreme Court vacancy), but he did an excellent job. He curbed the influence of the U.S. military, won the respect and cooperation of many Filipino leaders, and put down a rebellion under Emilio Aguinaldo against U.S. rule. He built English-language schools, improved sanitation, and became a genuinely popular figure with the Filipino people. Taft was appointed governor-general in 1901and served in that post until 1904, and for the first time he became nationally known.

SECRETARY OF WAR. President McKinley was assassinated in 1901. His successor was Taft's friend Theodore Roosevelt. Aware of Taft's desire for a Supreme Court seat, President Roosevelt offered to appoint him to the Supreme Court twice, in 1902 and 1906. In 1904, Roosevelt appointed him secretary of war. In this post Taft would still have responsibility for the Philippines but would also be available in Washington to help Roosevelt on other governmental missions. Taft served in this post until 1908. He continued to supervise the Philippines, but he also handled a variety of sensitive problems for Roosevelt. He went to Japan and carried on important talks about Japanese influence in the Far East. He agreed that the United States would not object to a Japanese presence in Korea if Japan did not complain about the U.S. presence in the Philippines. He also visited China twice and became more expert on Asian affairs than any other leading American. Taft supervised the beginning of the Panama Canal and for a brief period served as acting secretary of state. His good-natured, cautious personality made him an excellent diplomat. Occasionally he differed with the President, but on

This political cartoon by Clifford Berryman appeared in the Washington Post *on 15 March 1906. It shows Taft rejecting President Roosevelt's second offer of a seat on the Supreme Court.*

Berryman is best known for introducing the teddy bear as a permanent political symbol after Theodore Roosevelt refused to shoot a bear cub that had wandered into his hunting camp. Berryman was awarded the Pulitzer Prize in 1944.

Taft was appointed chief justice of the Supreme Court in 1921 by President Warren G. Harding. (Courtesy Collection of Charles E. Smith.)

Taft was appointed by President Roosevelt to succeed Elihu Root as secretary of war in 1904, and he served in that post until 1908. This portrait of Taft was painted during that period. (Courtesy National Archives.)

the whole his loyalty and devotion to duty won Roosevelt's increased respect.

THE ELECTION OF 1908. Roosevelt had promised in 1904 that he would not seek another term as president. He later regretted the promise, but he felt obliged to keep it. In 1908, therefore, he looked for a successor who was loyal and able to carry on his policies. Taft seemed the logical choice. Taft himself disliked the speechmaking and flattery that went with politics. He was reluctant to accept the nomination, but his brothers and Mrs. Taft, as well as Roosevelt, persuaded him to do so. The Republican convention nominated him, with James S. Sherman of New York as the vice presidential candidate. Taft was not an effective campaigner, but inspired by Roosevelt's popularity, he easily defeated the Democratic candidate, William Jennings Bryan.

PRESIDENT. Taft's goal as president was administrative. He did not expect to be a leader like Roosevelt, generating new policies and explaining them to the voters. He simply wanted to continue Roosevelt's foreign and domestic policies and execute them more thoroughly and efficiently. He

This group photograph was taken at the dedication of the building for the Pan American Union, which became the Organization of American States (OAS) in 1948. President Taft is in the center; on his left is the philanthropist Andrew Carnegie; on his right is Elihu Root. Fourth from the right is James Cardinal Gibbons, the second American cardinal. (Courtesy Library of Congress.)

expected to work through the Republican Party, and he expected other Republicans to cooperate with him. Unfortunately, his inexperience as a politician got in the way. He had little skill in cultivating the good will of persons with whom he disagreed and little understanding of the feelings of others. By his actions as president, he frequently made bitter enemies, especially among Republicans, without intending to do so. At the same time, he disliked interpersonal conflict and often put off decisions in the hope of avoiding it. A large part of his own party had turned against him before two years of his term had elapsed.

Taft's personality was frequently misunderstood. He was a large man, weighing more than three hundred pounds, who enjoyed the company of others and laughed frequently. Underneath the good nature, however, he was very sensitive to criticism. He carried grudges against his enemies and found it difficult to make up with them. His sensitivity deepened the divisions he created in the Republican Party.

THE PINCHOT-BALINGER AFFAIR. An early controversy that damaged Taft's image in his own party involved Roosevelt's conservation policies. Under Roosevelt, the Interior Department had set aside millions of acres of public land for conservation. Taft and his secretary of the interior, Richard A. Ballinger, both conservationists, were concerned that this action had been taken without proper authority from Congress. They felt that until Congress passed a more explicit law, some of this land should be offered for sale to private interests, and Ballinger took steps to do so.

Gifford Pinchot, chief of the Forest Service and a good friend of Roosevelt, protested this move. Specifically, he charged Ballinger with selling some Alaska lands fraudulently to an Eastern syndicate that wanted to develop coal deposits. Taft asked Attorney General George W. Wickersham to investigate, and the investigative report cleared Ballinger. Pinchot persisted with his charges, writing letters to the newspapers and to members of Congress. Taft resented his prolonging the controversy. In January 1910, he fired Pinchot. This act caused outrage among Roosevelt's admirers, the "progressive" Republicans. (Roosevelt himself was out of the country and was not involved in the controversy.) They urged Ballinger's dismissal as well. Taft refused, retaining Ballinger in office until 1911. In doing so, he opened a breach between his own conservative wing of the party and the progressive Republicans.

THE PAYNE-ALDRICH TARIFF. Another controversy early in Taft's term had similar effects. Taft had indicated during his election campaign that he favored a lowering of tariff rates. This was a popular position, especially with progressive Republicans and with Democrats, who felt that tariffs had been set too high because of business's excessive influence on Congress. Immediately after taking office in 1909, Taft called Congress into special session to write a new tariff. But he failed to offer a proposal of his own or even to state in general terms what sort of tariff he wanted. He made no attempt to rally public support for his views. Congress, left to itself, produced a bill that raised tariffs on many items instead of lowering them. Taft managed to secure a few reductions that he was interested in. On Philippine goods, for example, tariffs were almost eliminated. In general, however, the bill was not what Taft had favored, and many progressive Republicans expected him to veto it.

To their surprise, Taft signed the bill. His reasons for doing so were that he favored some provisions in it. He was tired of fighting over the bill and reluctant to begin the process again. Eager to gain the goodwill of the business-oriented Republicans who controlled Congress, he made speeches later in 1909 praising the new tariff. Republican progressives felt especially betrayed by this action. To the country as a whole, it suggested that Taft was a president who could not be trusted to keep his word.

ACHIEVEMENTS. Despite the charges of progressive Republicans that he was betraying Roosevelt's legacy, Taft did much to advance policies associated with Roosevelt. His Justice Department began more prosecutions against

TAFT'S DEFENSE OF THE PAYNE-ALDRICH TARIFF

. . . The Ways and Means Committee of the House, with Mr. Payne at its head, spent a full year in an investigation, assembling evidence in reference to the rates under the tariff, and devoted an immense amount of work in the study of the question where the tariff rates could be reduced and where they ought to be raised with a view to maintaining a reasonably protective rate, under the principles of the platform, for every industry that deserved protection. . . .

Mr. Payne reported a bill—the Payne Tariff bill—which went to the Senate and was amended in the Senate by increasing the duty on some things and decreasing it on others. The difference between the House bill and the Senate bill was very much less than the newspapers represented. . . .

Now, the promise of the Republican platform was not to revise everything downward, and in the speeches which have been taken as interpreting that platform, which I made in the campaign, I did not promise that everything should go downward. What I promised was, that there should be many decreases, and that in some few things increases would be found to be necessary; but that on the whole I conceived that the change of conditions would make the revision necessarily downward—and that, I contend, under the showing which I have made, has been the result of the Payne bill. I did not agree, nor did the Republican party agree, that we would reduce rates to such a point as to reduce prices by the introduction of foreign competition. That is what the free traders desire. That is what the revenue tariff reforms desire; but that is not what the Republican platform promised, and it is not what the Republican party wished to bring about. To repeat the statement with which I opened this speech, the proposition of the Republican party was to reduce rates so as to maintain a difference between the cost of production abroad and the cost of production here, insuring a reasonable profit to the manufacturer on all articles produced in this country; and the proposition to reduce rates and prevent their being excessive was to avoid the opportunity for monopoly and the suppression of competition, so that the excessive rates could be taken advantage of to force prices up. . . .

On the whole, however, I am bound to say that I think the Payne tariff bill is the best tariff bill that the Republican party ever passed. . . .

If the country desires free trade, and the country desires a revenue tariff and wishes the manufacturers all over the country to go out of business, and to have cheaper prices at the expense of the sacrifice of many of our manufacturing interests, then it ought to say so and ought to put the Democratic party in power if it thinks that party can be trusted to carry out any affirmative policy in favor of a revenue tariff. Certainly in the discussions in the Senate there was no great manifestation on the part of our Democratic friends in favor of reducing rates on necessities. They voted to maintain the tariff rates on everything that came from their particular sections. If we are to have free trade, certainly it can not be had through the maintenance of Republican majorities in the Senate and House and a Republican administration. . . .

• *The 1908 Republican platform had promised tariff "revision." Soon after taking office (1909), Taft called a special session of Congress to deal with the entire tariff issue.*

The House bill called for large rate reduction without abandoning the principle of protection for U.S. industries from foreign imports. In the Senate, however, more than 600 amendments were added. Many were carefully worded to conceal higher rates. Taft's approval of the law was widely viewed as a betrayal of his campaign promises, especially in the Middle West. The Payne-Aldrich Tariff (1909) began a major split within the Republican Party between the "progressives" and the "Old-Guard Republicans."

Special Message to Congress on the Income Tax

. . . The decision of the Supreme Court in the income-tax cases (1895) deprived the National Government of a power which, by reason of previous decisions of the court, it was generally supposed that Government had. It is undoubtedly a power the National Government ought to have. It might be indispensable to the nation's life in great crises. Although I have not considered a constitutional amendment as necessary to the exercise of certain phases of this power, a mature consideration has satisfied me that an amendment is the only proper course for its establishment to its full extent. I therefore recommend to the Congress that both Houses, by a two-thirds vote, shall propose an amendment to the Constitution conferring the power to levy an income tax upon the National Government without apportionment among the States in proportion to population.

This course is much to be preferred to the one proposed of reenacting a law once judicially declared to be unconstitutional. For the Congress to assume that the court will reverse itself, and to enact legislation on such an assumption, will not strengthen popular confidence in the stability of judicial construction of the Constitution. It is much wiser policy to accept the decision and remedy the defect by amendment in due and regular course.

Again, it is clear that by the enactment of the proposed law, the Congress will not be bringing money into the Treasury to meet the present deficiency, but by putting on the statute book a law already there and never repealed, will simply be suggesting to the executive officers of the Government their possible duty to invoke litigation. If the court should maintain its former view, no tax would be collected at all. If it should ultimately reverse itself, still no taxes would have been collected until after protracted delay.

It is said the difficulty and delay in securing the approval of three-fourths of the States will destroy all chance of adopting the amendment. Of course, no one can speak with certainty upon this point, but I have become convinced that a great majority of the people of this country are in favor of vesting the National Government with power to levy an income tax, and that they will secure the adoption of the amendment in the States, if proposed to them. . . .

• *The Constitution stated that: "No . . . direct Tax shall be laid, unless in proportion to the Census. . . ." What did this clause mean? Would a tax on income violate these words? Until the beginning of the twentieth century, the federal government had adequate funds—primarily from land sales and from tariff duties. As industrialization produced greedy people of great wealth and governmental services began to increase, progressives demanded a tax on income. Taft doubted the constitutionality of such an act—but he urged that the issue be referred to the states. Taft delivered this special message to Congress on 16 June 1909.*

The Sixteenth Amendment (The Income Tax Amendment) was proposed to the state legislatures on 12 July 1909 and declared ratified on 25 February 1913. The first income tax (1913) affected a tiny fraction of Americans who earned more than $4,000 a year. It began a momentous shift in the government revenue base from land sales and tariff duties to personal and corporate incomes.

business trusts than had been undertaken in the administration of Roosevelt, the so-called trust-buster. Taft also devised the strategy that led to successful enactment of a personal income tax. Democrats and progressive Republicans in Congress viewed this tax as a fairer way of raising money for the government than relying on the tariff. Taft agreed with them, but as a former judge he knew that the Supreme Court in 1895 had ruled an income tax unconstitutional and felt that Congress should not defy the Court. He persuaded them to pass a constitutional amendment legalizing the income tax, and in the meantime to impose a tax on corporations.

AMENDMENT XVI

The Congress shall have power to lay and collect taxes on incomes, from whatever source derived, without apportionment among the several States, and without regard to any census or enumeration.

• *For the complete text of the Constitution, see Volume 8.*

The achievement into which Taft put most effort was the passage in 1911 of a treaty guaranteeing free trade between the United States and Canada. Both Taft and Roosevelt favored this move, but the progressive Republicans, many of whom came from grain-producing states in the Midwest, opposed lowering tariffs on competing Canadian products. Taft used his influence as president to gain congressional approval for the treaty, but his victory was frustrated when political changes in Canada brought in a new government that rejected the agreement.

FOREIGN POLICY. Taft's greatest foreign policy challenge came in 1911 when revolution broke out in Mexico. For the last two years of his term Mexico was unstable and racked by a war that threatened U.S. business interests. In this case, Taft's inactivity served his country well. He resisted calls from both progressive and conservative Republicans for military action. At the end of his term, the United States was still uninvolved in the Mexican conflict. Elsewhere in the world, he was less successful. He devoted much time to negotiating with China to improve opportunities for U.S. business but accomplished little. He promoted U.S. trade with Latin America. On occasion, he sent U.S. troops into Central American countries to stop disorders that threatened Americans—for instance, in Nicaragua in 1911.

TAFT'S ESTRANGEMENT FROM ROOSEVELT. Taft had hoped, when he assumed the presidency, to carry on Roosevelt's policies and to win his approval. Instead, a coolness developed between the two friends that deepened into hostility. By 1912, they were open enemies. The process of estrangement was gradual. Immediately after Taft's inauguration, Roosevelt went abroad on a series of long trips and good-will tours to give Taft a feeling of freedom and to avoid stealing the spotlight from him. By 1910, however, he had become dissatisfied with Taft's policies and was expressing his feelings to close friends. Taft, he believed, was not aggressive enough and was too willing to cooperate with the most conservative elements of the party. "He has not the qualities that are needed at the moment," Roosevelt wrote.

When Roosevelt returned to the United States in June 1910, progressive Republicans visited him repeatedly to air their grievances against Taft. Taft wanted Roosevelt to express public support for his administration, and he was hurt when Roosevelt avoided doing so. He invited Roosevelt to visit him in the White House, but Roosevelt declined. Gradually Taft concluded that Roosevelt was planning to run against him in 1912 for the Republican presidential nomination. He had not planned to

Taft (right) and Theodore Roosevelt were close for many years, but their friendship fell apart when Roosevelt's candidacy for the Progressive (Bull Moose) Party cost Taft his reelection. According to Tim Taylor in The Book of Presidents, *they met by chance in the dining room of the Blackstone Hotel in Chicago on 5 May 1918 and shook hands. "I've seen old Taft," said Roosevelt later, "and we're in perfect harmony on everything." Eight months later, Taft attended Roosevelt's funeral.* (Courtesy Library of Congress.)

seek a second term, but now, angry at Roosevelt's behavior, he decided to compete against his old friend for the nomination if Roosevelt chose to run.

In 1911, the break between the two men became public. Taft's administration filed an antitrust suit against the United States Steel Corporation that charged, among other things, that U.S. Steel's purchase of the Tennessee Coal and Iron Company in 1908, approved by the Roosevelt administration, had been illegal. The mention of Roosevelt's administration in the suit was not authorized by Taft, but it infuriated the former president. Roosevelt responded with an angry defense of his policy in a magazine article. In February 1912, he announced that he was running for president.

ELECTION OF 1912. The battle for the Republican nomination in 1912 was extremely bitter. Taft, angry at Roosevelt's challenge, mobilized all his friends among conservative Republicans. Privately and publicly Roosevelt began criticizing Taft as a lazy, indecisive, inactive president—a "fathead," a "flubdub," a "floppy-souled creature." Taft at first did not respond, but when Roosevelt advocated removing judges who made unpopular decisions, Taft was stirred into action. He toured the country speaking against the progressives—radicals, demagogues, and neurotics, he called them. Roosevelt was clearly more popular with the mass of Republicans, but Taft's supporters controlled the party machinery, and he defeated Roosevelt for the nomination.

Roosevelt promptly quit the Republican Party, formed a party of his own, the Progressive (Bull Moose) Party and ran for president on an independent ticket. The effect of this action was to divide the Republican vote and give an advantage in most states to the Democratic nominee, Governor Woodrow Wilson of New Jersey. Taft, aware that he would probably lose, hardly campaigned at all in the fall election, except for a few speeches defending his moderate conservative policy. He was satisfied to lose as long as Roosevelt did not win. In the final results, Wilson was elected with a large majority in the Electoral College. Taft won only two states, Utah and Vermont.

PROFESSOR OF LAW. Taft left the White House with relief. He was glad to accept the Kent Chair of Constitutional Law at Yale University. He spent the next eight years of his life teaching, writing, and lecturing on public issues. He had no further interest in political office; however, when the United States entered World War I, Taft became a speaker for the Wilson administration, defending U.S. involvement. In 1918, President Wilson appointed him to the National War Labor Board. He became partly reconciled with Theodore Roosevelt before Roosevelt's death in 1919.

CHIEF JUSTICE. In 1921, the newly elected Republican president, Warren G. Harding of Ohio, appointed Taft chief justice of the United States to succeed Edward D. White. Taft accepted eagerly. It was the peak of his career. He remains the only person in U.S. history to serve as both president and chief justice. As chief justice, Taft was aggressive and decisive in a way he had never been as president. The difference was that he found the Supreme Court pleasant and genuinely enjoyed his work. His main contributions were administrative. He persuaded Congress to simplify the appeals process and reduce the Court's caseload. He led the fight for the Court to have a building of its own, overcoming the resistance of several other justices. His effort was successful, although he did not live to see the new building completed. Using diplomacy and his good nature, he reduced personal tensions among some of the other justices and made the Court's atmosphere both friendlier and more efficient.

In his nine years of service, Taft wrote 253 decisions, about one sixth of all the decisions handed down by the Court during that time. His opinions were generally conservative and legalistic. In *Bailey v. Drexel Furniture Co.* (1922), he ruled that the Child Labor Act of 1919 was an unconstitutional invasion of states' rights, regardless of its "good purpose." His most important decision, *Myers v. United States* (1926), upheld the president's power to remove a postmaster without the consent

William Howard Taft became chief justice of the United States on 30 June 1921. He resigned on 3 February 1930 due to illness. (Courtesy Library of Congress.)

"None of Taft's predecessors, with the possible exception of (John) Marshall, entertained so expansive a view of the chief justiceship, or used it so effectively on so many fronts. Taft was a great administrator, a great judicial architect, a skillful harmonizer of human relations. Yet he is not commonly considered a great Chief Justice." Alpheus Thomas Mason, "Taft, William Howard," Encyclopedia of the American Constitution, *edited by Leonard W. Levy, Kenneth L. Karst, and Dennis J. Mahoney.*

of the Senate. This decision also pronounced unconstitutional the Tenure of Office Act of 1867. This had been the basis for the impeachment trial of President Andrew Johnson.

Taft was in poor health, due to obesity and a heart condition, during his last few years on the Supreme Court. He resigned from the Court in February 1930 and died in Washington one month later, on 8 March 1930. He was the first president to be buried in Arlington National Cemetery, Arlington, Virginia.

"We call you Chief Justice still—for we cannot give up the title by which we have known you all these later years and which you have made dear to us. We cannot let you leave us without trying to tell you how dear you have made it. You came to us from achievement in other fields and with the prestige of the illustrious place that you lately had held and you showed us in new form your voluminous capacity for getting work done, your humor that smoothed the tough places, your golden heart that brought you love from every side and most of all from your brethren whose tasks you have made happy and light. We grieve at your illness, but your spirit has given an impulse that will abide whether you are with us or away."

• *After Taft's son, Robert, delivered his father's resignation to President Herbert Hoover, Oliver Wendell Holmes wrote the above note to Taft on behalf of the Supreme Court.*

This picture of Chief Justice Taft (right) was taken with Justice Oliver Wendell Holmes in 1926 on Holmes's 85th birthday. (Courtesy Library of Congress.)

A tribute that would have greatly pleased Taft came from humorist Will Rogers: "It's great to be great but it's greater to be human. He was our great fellow because there was more of him to be human. We are parting with three hundred pounds of solid charity to everyone, and love and affection for all his fellow men."

Vice President

James Schoolcraft Sherman (1855–1912)

Chronological Events

1855	Born, Utica, New York, 24 October
1878	Graduated from Hamilton College, Clinton, New York
1884	Elected mayor of Utica, New York
1886	Elected to U.S. House of Representatives
1908	Elected vice president
1912	Died, Utica, New York, 30 October

Biography

Since James Schoolcraft Sherman's grandfather ran a glass factory and his father operated a food canning factory, Sherman naturally adopted pro-business positions when he entered politics. A noted debater at Hamilton College, Sherman became a successful lawyer. At age 29, he won election as mayor of Utica, New York and spent the rest of his life in politics.

Elected to the U.S. House of Representatives in 1886, Sherman fought for high protective tariffs and the gold standard. Widely known as "Sunny Jim" for his disposition, Sherman became a leader among House Republicans. Several Speakers of the House appreciated his parliamentary skills and relied on Sherman to preside in their absence. But he failed to win election as Speaker himself.

Sherman's chairmanship of the Republican Congressional Campaign Committee in 1906 earned him recognition for his organizing and fund-raising abilities. In 1908, William Howard Taft won the Republican presidential nomination as a progressive. To satisfy party conservatives, the vice presidential nomination went to Sherman.

Once he won the election, Taft faced the difficult task of replacing Theodore Roosevelt in the White House. When Taft sought reduced tariff rates, congressional Republicans responded with the even higher Payne-Aldrich Tariff. Always a high-tariff advocate, Sherman urged the President to sign the tariff bill, a move that offended and alienated the progressives.

As Taft grew more conservative, he became closer to his vice president. Beneath his sunny exterior, Sherman was a tough politician who prompted Taft to take firm stands. Sherman urged the President to cut off the patronage appointments of any Republicans who opposed the Payne-Aldrich Tariff. In 1910, he supported Taft's decision to fire the head of the U.S. Forest Service, Gifford Pinchot, a close friend of Theodore Roosevelt.

The widening split within the Republican Party encouraged Theodore Roosevelt to leave retirement and challenge Taft for the Republican nomination in 1912. When the Republican Party renominated Taft and Sherman, Roosevelt bolted to lead the new Progressive (Bull Moose) Party. By then, Sherman was seriously ill with kidney disease and unable to campaign. His death in October left Taft without a running mate. Taft finished last in the three-way race, losing to the Democratic candidate, Woodrow Wilson. Before the Electoral College met, the Republicans chose Columbia University President Nicholas Murray Butler as Sherman's replacement.

THE CABINET

SECRETARY OF STATE
Philander C. Knox, 1909

SECRETARY OF WAR
Jacob M. Dickinson, 1909
Henry L. Stimson, 1911

SECRETARY OF THE TREASURY
Franklin MacVeagh, 1909

POSTMASTER GENERAL
Frank H. Hitchcock, 1909

ATTORNEY GENERAL
George W. Wichersham, 1909

SECRETARY OF THE NAVY
George von L. Meyer, 1909

SECRETARY OF THE INTERIOR
Richard A. Ballinger, 1909
Walter Lowrie Fisher, 1911

SECRETARY OF AGRICULTURE
James Wilson, 1909

SECRETARY OF COMMERCE AND LABOR
Charles Nagel, 1909

(Courtesy National Archives.)

George von L. Meyer (1858–1918). Meyer was appointed secretary of the navy by President William Howard Taft in 1909. He had previously served as U.S. minister to Italy (1900–1905), U.S. minister to Russia (1905–1907), and postmaster general (1907–1909).

Meyer was an effective administrator. As postmaster general during Theodore Roosevelt's administration, he established postal savings banks, started the special-delivery system, and extended the parcel-post system.

President Taft retained Meyer in his cabinet and appointed him secretary of the navy. Meyer greatly increased the efficiency of the Navy Department. He improved the techniques and procedures of operating naval guns and reorganized the navy yard to meet the needs of the fleet rather than that of the local constituencies. He also instituted the system of appointing naval assistants to keep him and future navy secretaries better informed.

The Cabinet

(Courtesy Library of Congress.)

Philander C. Knox (1853–1921). Knox was appointed secretary of state by President William Howard Taft in 1909. He had previously served as attorney general in the administrations of William McKinley and Theodore Roosevelt. He also served as a senator from Pennsylvania in the U.S. Senate (1904–1909).

As secretary of state, Knox implemented the U.S. foreign policy called "dollar diplomacy" in the Far East and then in Latin America. This plan promoted political reform through business loans rather than through direct military assistance. Knox also reorganized the State Department. He created the new offices of counselor, director of the consular service, and resident diplomatic officer.

In 1917, Knox was reelected to the U.S. Senate, where he became one of the chief opponents of President Woodrow Wilson's foreign policies. Knox, together with Senator Henry Cabot Lodge of Massachusetts, led the fight against the ratification of the Treaty of Versailles. The Senate rejected the treaty in 1919 and again in 1920.

CHRONOLOGICAL EVENTS

2 June 1861	Helen (Nellie) Herron born	1 August 1891	Daughter, Helen, born
19 June 1886	Helen Herron married William Howard Taft	20 September 1897	Son, Charles, born
8 September 1889	Son, Robert, born	8 March 1930	William Howard Taft died
		22 May 1943	Helen Taft died

Robert Taft is shown (right) in the picture of the Taft family taken on the White House lawn shortly after his father's Inauguration. (Courtesy Library of Congress.)

Nellie Taft was the first wife of a president to ride down Pennsylvania Avenue next to her husband on Inauguration Day. Two months later, she suffered a stroke while on the presidential yacht and her speech became impaired. On a trip to Japan, she had become very fond of Japanese cherry trees. She arranged for the planting of the 3,000 cherry trees along the Tidal Basin. She and the wife of the Japanese ambassador personally planted the first trees on 27 March 1912.

The Tafts celebrated their 25th wedding anniversary with a memorable party at the White House for several thousand guests. Mrs. Taft had attended a similar party for President and Mrs. Hayes when she was 17 years old.

Their daughter, Helen, returned from college to help her mother when she was ill. She later received a doctorate in history from Yale University and became dean of Bryn Mawr College. Charles served in World War I and later received his law degree from Yale. He was active in Cincinnati politics, and he once ran for governor of Ohio.

Robert graduated first in his class from Harvard Law School, and he served in the U.S. Senate from 1938 to 1953. He sponsored the Taft-Hartley Act and became known as "Mr. Republican."

President Taft's son, Robert (right), lost the Republican nomination for president to Dwight D. Eisenhower (left) in Chicago, July 1952. (Courtesy Dwight D. Eisenhower Library.)

PLACES

William Howard Taft National Historic Site

2038 Auburn Avenue • Cincinnati, Ohio 45219-3025 • Tel: (513) 684-3262

Located approximately one mile south of U.S. 52. Open daily from 10 A.M. to 4 P.M. Closed Thanksgiving, Christmas, and New Year's Day. No admission fee. Group tours available; must write or call in advance. The house is wheelchair accessible. There is an elevator to exhibits on the second floor. Administered by the National Park Service, U.S. Department of the Interior.

The William Howard Taft National Historic Site is the only memorial to the twenty-seventh President of the United States and the tenth Chief Justice of the Supreme Court, the two highest offices in the nation. (Courtesy William Howard Taft National Historic Site.)

The William Howard Taft National Historic Site contains a three-story home on three acres of land. Taft's father, Alphonso, purchased it in 1851 and built a three-story addition. Taft was born six years later, in the first-floor bedroom. He lived there until his marriage to Helen Herron in 1886.

The home remained in the Taft family until 1899. In 1938, with the establishment of the William Howard Taft Memorial Association, a movement was begun to save the deteriorating house from demolition. The association, under the leadership of Charles Phelps Taft II, son of the President, gained control of the house and grounds in 1961. Eight years later, Congress designated them a National Historic Site. Restored by the National Park Service, the site was opened to the public in 1988.

The letters of Taft's mother to her family in Massachusetts were used as a guide in the restoration of the house. They provided a detailed account of decorating plans, home improvements, and furniture purchases. Four of the restored rooms depict the Taft family home setting during President Taft's boyhood; the rest of the three-story house contains exhibits that chart his life.

Woodrow Wilson

CHRONOLOGICAL EVENTS

28 December 1856	Born, Staunton, Virginia
18 June 1879	Graduated from College of New Jersey (now Princeton University)
19 October 1882	Admitted to bar, Atlanta, Georgia
23 January 1885	Published *Congressional Government*
June 1886	Received Ph.D. from Johns Hopkins University, Baltimore, Maryland
9 June 1902	Elected president of Princeton University
20 October 1910	Resigned as president of Princeton University
8 November 1910	Elected governor of New Jersey
5 November 1912	Elected president
4 March 1913	Inaugurated president
3 October 1913	Signed Underwood Tariff Act
23 December 1913	Signed Glass-Owen Federal Reserve Act
2–4 August 1914	World War I began in Europe
26 September 1914	Signed Federal Trade Commission Act
15 October 1914	Signed Clayton Antitrust Act
7 May 1915	Sinking of the *Lusitania*
7 November 1916	Reelected president
5 March 1917	Inaugurated president
1 March 1917	Zimmermann telegram published
2 April 1917	Delivered war message to Congress
6 April 1917	Signed declaration of war against Germany
8 January 1918	Delivered "Fourteen Points" speech
16 May 1918	Signed Sedition Act
11 November 1918	Armistice signed, ending World War I
28 June 1919	Treaty of Versailles signed
2 October 1919	Suffered stroke
10 December 1920	Awarded Nobel Peace Prize
3 February 1924	Died, Washington, D.C.

BIOGRAPHY

Woodrow Wilson, who was president during World War I, came to the presidency from an unusual background. He was a college professor and president, a writer, and a superb speaker, confident of his own ideas and his own righteousness. His eight years as president saw some major achievements, including the acceptance by the United States of an important international role. Many historians have ranked him as one of the great presidents. But his administration also saw some failures, caused in part by Wilson's own arrogance.

CHILDHOOD. Thomas Woodrow Wilson (he dropped his first name after graduating from college) was born 28 December 1856 in Staunton, Virginia. His father, Joseph Ruggles Wilson, was a popular, intellectual Presbyterian minister, the son of immigrants from Northern Ireland, known for his excellent sermons. His English-born mother, Jessie Woodrow Wilson, was also a strong personality. There was a substantial British element in Wilson's upbringing. His family subscribed to British periodicals, and young Wilson was a strong admirer of the British Parliament and the British navy.

EDUCATION. Wilson's childhood coincided with the Civil War and Reconstruction. He lived in a series of Southern towns where his father pastored Presbyterian churches—Augusta, Georgia; Columbia, South Carolina; and Wilmington, North Carolina; none of them close to the war zone. Opportunities for schooling were limited, and Wilson was taught at home by his family. He did not learn to read until he was 12 years old; historians have suspected that he had dyslexia, a disease that caused a great difficulty in reading and writing. In his teens he attended an academy in Columbia, where he was an average student. At the age of 16 he entered Davidson College, a Presbyterian institution in North Carolina. Homesick, he dropped out after a year and rejoined his family in Wilmington.

PRINCETON. In 1875, Wilson entered Princeton, at that time also a strongly Presbyterian college. There he was strikingly successful, especially in outside activities. He became a skilled debater in the American Whig Society, a student club, and founded a society of his own, modeled on the British Parliament, to discuss public issues. He read widely in history and political science, and his grades were excellent in these subjects. He also served for a year as editor of the student newspaper, *The Princetonian*. By graduation in 1879, he was one of the best-known and most popular students in his class.

LAWYER. With his serious interest in public issues, Wilson hoped someday to be elected to public office. His dream was to be a U.S. senator. He decided to become a lawyer as a way of getting into politics. In 1879, he enrolled at the University of Virginia to study law. Poor health compelled him to leave in 1880 without a degree. He completed his studies at his family's home in Wilmington. He selected Atlanta as a place to practice and was admitted to the Georgia bar in 1882. His practice, however, was unsuccessful. He read and wrote articles on public questions, but made little money. The one benefit of his year in Atlanta was that he met his wife, Ellen Axson of Rome, Georgia, whom he married in 1885.

POLITICAL SCIENTIST. Frustrated in law, Wilson turned to a profession in which he could make a living reading and writing about politics: graduate study and college teaching. He entered the Johns Hopkins University in Baltimore and graduated in 1886 with a Ph.D. in political science. (Wilson remains the only president to have earned this degree.) While still in graduate school, he published his first major book, *Congressional Government,* which received good reviews. From then on, his rise in the academic world was rapid. He taught political science and history at Bryn Mawr College from 1885 to 1888, at Wesleyan College in Connecticut from 1888 to 1890, and at Princeton University from 1890 to 1902. At the same time, he turned out many books and articles, including his major work, *The State* (1889), winning a national reputation in his field. He was much in demand as a lecturer and was considered one of the best speakers in the United States.

PRESIDENT OF PRINCETON. In 1902, Wilson was elected president of Princeton to succeed the retiring president, James Patton. He was the first nonclergyman to hold the office, and the first Southerner. He served eight years (1902–1910) as president. These were years of tremendous growth in the college, and Wilson decisively influenced that growth. His accomplishments included reform of the curriculum and improvement of the faculty by bringing in young scholars from other colleges. He built two major science buildings and appointed the noted architect Ralph Adams Cram to supervise the overall development of the campus.

Wilson's presidency is also remembered for two policy battles in which he made bitter enemies because of his stubbornness and refusal to compromise. He lost both battles. The first, in 1906, concerned the student eating clubs on campus. These were private clubs, socially exclusive and lavishly furnished, for juniors and seniors from wealthy families. Wilson proposed replacing them with a quadrangle system similar to that of the British universities, in which students of all four academic classes would live in dormitories together and eat together. Wealthy alumni and conservatives on the faculty united to defeat Wilson's plan. This controversy had a strong effect on Wilson's thinking. He came to see himself as an enemy of rich, snobbish, powerful people. His political views began to become much more sympathetic to the progressives, who questioned the power of rich men and business interests.

From 1908 to 1910, Wilson was involved in a long controversy with the board of trustees and with some of the faculty that finally became so bitter that he had to resign. The dispute centered on the location of a new graduate school campus. This was a fairly trivial subject, but Wilson was absolutely insistent on having his own way and defended his views in passionate and emotional language. His opponent, Dean Andrew West of the Graduate College, was equally stubborn. Some historians have attributed Wilson's unreasonable attitude at this time to a minor stroke he may have suffered in 1906, which changed his personality in subtle ways. The medical evidence is not conclusive.

GOVERNOR. Increasingly uncomfortable at Princeton, Wilson began looking toward the field of politics. Since 1906 the influential Democratic editor of *Harper's Weekly*, George M. Harvey, had admired him and viewed him as a possible presidential candidate. Early in 1910, Harvey, acting on his own, approached New Jersey Democratic leaders to secure their support for Wilson as a candidate for governor that year. Harvey explained that Wilson would seek the governorship as a stepping stone to the presidency. James Smith of Newark, the Democratic boss, agreed as long as Wilson promised not to disturb his political machine. Wilson agreed, and in July 1910, he announced his candidacy. He was nominated in September and resigned as president of Princeton in October. After a vigorous campaign, he was elected in November.

To create the image of an independent progressive, Wilson as governor turned against the party bosses such as Smith who had given him the nomination. He persuaded the legislature to pass major bills reforming the political process. He also secured legislation to control the powerful oil companies and to provide workers' compensation (payments for injured workers). His attention, however, was focused on the presidential contest in 1912. Late in 1911, he began a nationwide speaking tour to win support from Democrats across the country with his thrilling speeches.

THE 1912 CAMPAIGN. Wilson faced three strong opponents for the Democratic nomination. The nominating convention, held in Baltimore, Maryland, lasted for days. Wilson finally won on the forty-sixth ballot over his leading rival, Speaker of the House James Beauchamp (Champ) Clark of Missouri. Support from the three-time Democratic presidential candidate William Jennings Bryan, who was still popular in the party, made Wilson's victory possible.

In the general election, Wilson's chances were better than those of any Democrat for 20 years. Republican voters were split. Some backed President William Howard Taft, who was a candidate for reelection, but many others favored former president Theodore Roosevelt, who was running on a third-party Progressive ticket (the Bull

Woodrow Wilson received telegrams congratulating him on his election to the presidency. He was in Sea Girt, New Jersey, which was then the official residence of New Jersey governors. (Courtesy Library of Congress.)

Moose Party). Wilson campaigned energetically in favor of reducing the influence of big business and passing laws to benefit working people. He called this program the "New Freedom." At election time, as expected, the Republicans' vote was divided between Roosevelt and Taft. Wilson, with only 42 percent of the popular vote, won a large majority in the Electoral College. He became the first Democratic president since Grover Cleveland.

PRESIDENCY. Wilson came to the presidency better prepared than almost any other president since the founding of the country. He had studied the presidency and its powers all his adult life, and he knew exactly what he wanted to do. His idea was that the president should be a leader on the British parliamentary model, with a carefully crafted plan of legislation that he would put through with the aid of his party. Knowing his own skill as a speaker, Wilson expected to make many major speeches as president. He revived the custom, inactive for more than a century, of presenting presidential messages to Congress in person as speeches rather than written documents.

DOMESTIC POLICY. The first two years of Wilson's presidency were very productive. In keeping with his campaign speeches, he developed reform bills on a number of economic problems and then used his persuasive speaking ability and influence with congressional Democrats to put them through Congress.

Two pieces of legislation were especially important. The Underwood Tariff (1913), named for its sponsor, Senator Oscar W. Underwood of Alabama, systematically lowered or eliminated tariffs on many imported goods. To make up for the loss of revenue, Congress imposed a modest federal income tax, the first in U.S. history, imposed only on the very rich.

The Glass-Owen Act (1913), sponsored by Representative Carter Glass of Virginia and Senator Robert L. Owen of Oklahoma, reformed the U.S. banking system by creating a system of federal superbanks, the Federal Reserve, with sole power to issue money. The Federal Reserve was conceived as a device to regulate the economy through government action rather than leaving it to private interests. Since 1913 it has evolved into the principal regulator of domestic economic matters.

The Clayton Antitrust Act (1914) and the Federal Trade Commission Act (1914), also sponsored by Wilson, imposed some new restrictions on the power of big corporations, but they were not aggressively antibusiness. Instead, they completed the reforms begun 10 years earlier by Theodore

In his first Inaugural Address, Woodrow Wilson restated the philosophy of the New Freedom, which he had often discussed during his campaign. The historian Henry Steele Commager said, "The address is one of the most notable statements of democratic faith in our political literature, and for eloquence compares favorably with Jefferson's First Inaugural and Lincoln's Second Inaugural." (Courtesy Library of Congress.)

FIRST INAUGURAL ADDRESS

. . . Our life contains every great thing, and contains it in rich abundance.

But the evil has come with the good, and much fine gold has been corroded. With riches has come inexcusable waste. We have squandered a great part of what we might have used, and have not stopped to conserve the exceeding bounty of nature, without which our genius for enterprise would have been worthless and impotent, scorning to be careful, shamefully prodigal as well as admirably efficient. We have been proud of our industrial achievements, but we have not hitherto stopped thoughtfully enough to count the human cost, the cost of lives snuffed out, of energies overtaxed and broken, the fearful physical and spiritual cost to the men and women and children upon whom the dead weight and burden of it all has fallen pitilessly the years through. The groans and agony of it all had not yet reached our ears, the solemn, moving undertone of our life, coming up out of the mines and factories, and out of every home where the struggle had its intimate and familiar seat. With the great Government went many deep secret things which we too long delayed to look into and scrutinize with candid, fearless eyes. The great Government we loved has too often been made use of for private and selfish purposes, and those who used it had forgotten the people. . . .

There has been something crude and heartless and unfeeling in our haste to succeed and be great. Our thought has been "Let every man look out for himself, let every generation look out for itself," while we reared giant machinery which made it impossible that any but those who stood at the levers of control should have a chance to look out for themselves. We had not forgotten our morals. We remembered well enough that we had set up a policy which was meant to serve the humblest as well as the most powerful, with an eye single to the standards of justice and fair play, and remembered it with pride. But we were very heedless and in a hurry to be great. . . .

Roosevelt. Business interests agreed to large parts of both of them.

Wilson was a reformer with regard to economic questions but much less so on social questions. With his Southern background, he was sympathetic to Democratic politicians who wanted racial segregation in government offices. Under Wilson, federal employees in the Treasury and the Post Office departments were segregated by race. Employees who protested were dismissed. African American leaders spoke out against the policy, but they were not influential enough to have it changed.

Two years later, as the presidential election of 1916 approached, Wilson sponsored more reforms. Most of these were designed to appeal to the Progressives who had voted for Roosevelt in 1912 and to persuade them to support Wilson for reelection. He appointed his Progressive economic adviser, Louis D. Brandeis, to the Supreme Court, a move of great symbolic significance, since Brandeis was not only a thorough Progressive but also the first Jew to sit on the Court. Wilson backed legislation to end child labor in factories (the law was later held unconstitutional by the Supreme Court), to limit railroad employees' work days to eight hours, to increase taxes on the rich, and to provide workers' compensation for federal employees. These measures served their purpose, attracting Progressive support and contributing to Wilson's reelection. But by this time, Wilson's attention was focused largely on foreign policy questions.

FOREIGN POLICY. Wilson sent troops to take over the governments of Haiti and the Dominican Republic during his presidency, and he maintained a small armed force in Nicaragua. Both Wilson and his secretary of state, William Jennings Bryan, disliked U.S. intervention on principle. However, they shared the view, common to many Americans, that Latin Americans were disorderly and often incapable of governing themselves. Moreover, they felt a need to protect the U.S. presence in Panama, where the interoceanic canal was being finished. The actions demonstrated Wilson's willingness to intervene in other countries' affairs, given an opportunity.

U.S. intervention was less successful in Mexico. Wilson disapproved of the new president, Victoriano Huerta, who had taken power in a coup in which his predecessor, Francisco Madero, was killed. To express U.S. disfavor, Wilson refused to recognize the new regime unless Huerta promised to step down in favor of an elected successor. Huerta at first indicated he would do so and then changed his mind. Wilson, furious, determined to remove him as head of Mexico. In 1914, Wilson seized on an incident in Tampico, where Mexican authorities had arrested U.S. sailors, to demand an apology. When Huerta refused to give it, Wilson sent Marines to occupy the chief Mexican port of Veracruz. U.S. public opinion was generally skeptical of the need for this action. Mediation by other Latin American countries kept the situation from developing into war. A few months later, Huerta's government fell, and he fled the country. Wilson then removed the troops.

Huerta's fall was followed by a civil war between President Venustiano Carranza and one of his generals, Pancho Villa. In this conflict Wilson's government supported first Villa and then Carranza. Villa's forces, angry at the withdrawal of support, in January 1916, began killing Americans at random in Mexico and across the border in the United States. Wilson, in response, sent an army expedition under General John J. Pershing to capture Villa in Mexico. The U.S. forces penetrated deep into Mexico and were involved in several shooting incidents with Villa's forces. The Carranza government protested this violation of Mexican sovereignty. As Villa's raids continued, Wilson was ready to ask Congress for a declaration of war against Mexico, but protests from a large number of Americans who wanted peace changed his mind. At the beginning of 1917, he withdrew the forces from Mexico because it now seemed likely that the United States would soon be involved in a European war.

THE EUROPEAN WAR AND U.S. NEUTRALITY. Wilson's greatest foreign policy problem was World War I, which broke out in Europe in the summer of 1914 between the Central Powers, led by Germany, and the Allies, led by Great Britain and France. Wilson was determined that the United States remain neutral and not get involved in the fighting. Neutrality proved hard to maintain, however, since U.S. companies traded actively with both Germany and Great Britain. Each of these powers wanted to prevent U.S. supplies from reaching the other. Great Britain used its fleet to blockade Germany, while German submarines, used for the first time in warfare, threatened ships carrying goods to Great Britain. In May 1915, a German submarine sank the British transatlantic liner *Lusitania* off the British coast, killing almost 1,200 passengers, including 128 Americans. The U.S. public was outraged by this act. Some Americans, including Theodore Roosevelt, wanted to declare war on Germany. Wilson, after a few more similar incidents, demanded that the German Government stop this practice, and Germany agreed to do so.

At the same time, U.S. neutrality began tilting more and more toward Great Britain. In 1915, the government allowed New York bankers to make a large loan to Great Britain and France. Wilson, insisting that the United States was "too proud to fight" with Germany, at the same time sponsored measures to strengthen the armed forces in case the United States became involved in the war.

ELECTION of 1916. In 1916, Wilson ran for reelection against a reunited Republican Party, led by a New York Progressive, Charles Evans Hughes. The Democratic Party used the slogan "He kept us out of war" to appeal to German Americans, Irish Americans, and others who opposed war against Germany. Hughes, on the other hand, urged a tougher anti-German position, which many voters found attractive. Wilson won the election by an extremely narrow margin. The shift of 1,500 votes in California would have elected Hughes.

THE END OF NEUTRALITY. Three events in 1917 radically changed U.S. public opinion and generated strong feeling against Germany. In January, Germany announced that it was going to resume unrestricted submarine warfare. The following month British intelligence intercepted the Zimmermann Telegram from German Foreign Secretary Arthur Zimmermann to the German minister in Mexico. It offered Carranza's government the southwestern United States as a reward for helping Germany win the war if the United States should enter it. In March, German submarines began sinking U.S. merchant ships, resulting in heavy loss of life. Wilson felt that he had to respond to the German threat.

Reluctantly, on 2 April, he asked Congress for a declaration of war. Germany, he said in his speech to Congress, was engaged in "a war against mankind." The United States had to fight to "make the world safe for democracy. . . . We are but one of the champions of the rights of mankind." Congress voted for war.

THE ZIMMERMANN TELEGRAM

BERLIN, JANUARY 19, 1917

On the first of February we intend to begin submarine warfare unrestricted. In spite of this it is our intention to keep neutral the United States of America.

If this attempt is not successful we propose an alliance on the following basis with Mexico: That we shall make war together and together make peace. We shall give general financial support, and it is understood that Mexico is to reconquer the lost territory in New Mexico, Texas, and Arizona. The details are left for your settlement.

You are instructed to inform the President of Mexico of the above in the greatest confidence as soon as it is certain that there will be an outbreak of war with the United States. . . .

Please call to the attention of the President of Mexico that the employment of ruthless submarine warfare now promises to compel England to make peace in a few months.

Zimmermann

Declaration of War

. . . The present German submarine warfare against commerce is a warfare against mankind.

It is a war against all nations. American ships have been sunk, American lives taken, in ways which it has stirred us very deeply to learn of, but the ships and people of other neutral and friendly nations have been sunk and overwhelmed in the waters in the same way. There has been no discrimination. The challenge is to all mankind. Each nation must decide for itself how it will meet it. The choice we make for ourselves must be made with a moderation of counsel and a temperateness of judgment befitting our character and our motives as a nation. We must put excited feelings away. Our motive will not be revenge or the victorious assertion of the physical might of the nation, but only the vindication of right, of human right, of which we are only a single champion.

When I addressed the Congress on the twenty-sixth of February last I thought that it would suffice to assert our neutral rights with arms, our right to use the seas against unlawful interference, our right to keep our people safe against unlawful violence. But armed neutrality, it now appears, is impracticable. Because submarines are in effect outlaws when used as the German submarines have been used against merchant shipping, it is impossible to defend ships against their attacks as the law of nations has assumed that merchantmen would defend themselves against privateers or cruisers, visible craft giving chase upon the open sea. . . . There is one choice we cannot make, we are incapable of making: we will not choose the path of submission and suffer the most sacred rights of our Nation and our people to be ignored or violated. The wrongs against which we now array ourselves are no common wrongs; they cut to the very roots of human life.

With a profound sense of the solemn and even tragical character of the step I am taking and the grave responsibilities which it involves, but in unhesitating obedience to what I deem my constitutional duty, I advise that the Congress declare the recent course of the Imperial German Government to be in fact nothing less than war against the government and people of the United States; that it formally accept the status of belligerent which has thus been thrust upon it; and that it take immediate steps not only to put the country in a more thorough state of defense but also to exert all its power and employ all its resources to bring the Government of the German Empire to terms and end the war. . . .

We are glad, now that we see the facts with no veil of false pretense about them, to fight thus for the ultimate peace of the world and for the liberation of its peoples, the German peoples included: for the rights of nations great and small and the privilege of men everywhere to choose their way of life and of obedience. The world must be made safe for democracy. Its peace must be planted upon the tested foundations of political liberty. We have no selfish ends to serve. We desire no conquest, no dominion. We seek no indemnities for ourselves, no material compensation for the sacrifices we shall freely make. We are but one of the champions of the rights of mankind. We shall be satisfied when those rights have been made as secure as the faith and the freedom of nations can make them. . . .

• *President Wilson concluded that his previous plan for armed neutrality was not practical, and he delivered a special message to Congress on 2 April 1917. It was one of his greatest speeches and one of the great speeches of the twentieth century. He noted that, "It is a fearful thing to lead this great peaceful people into war, into the most terrible and disastrous of all wars, civilization itself seeming to be in the balance."*

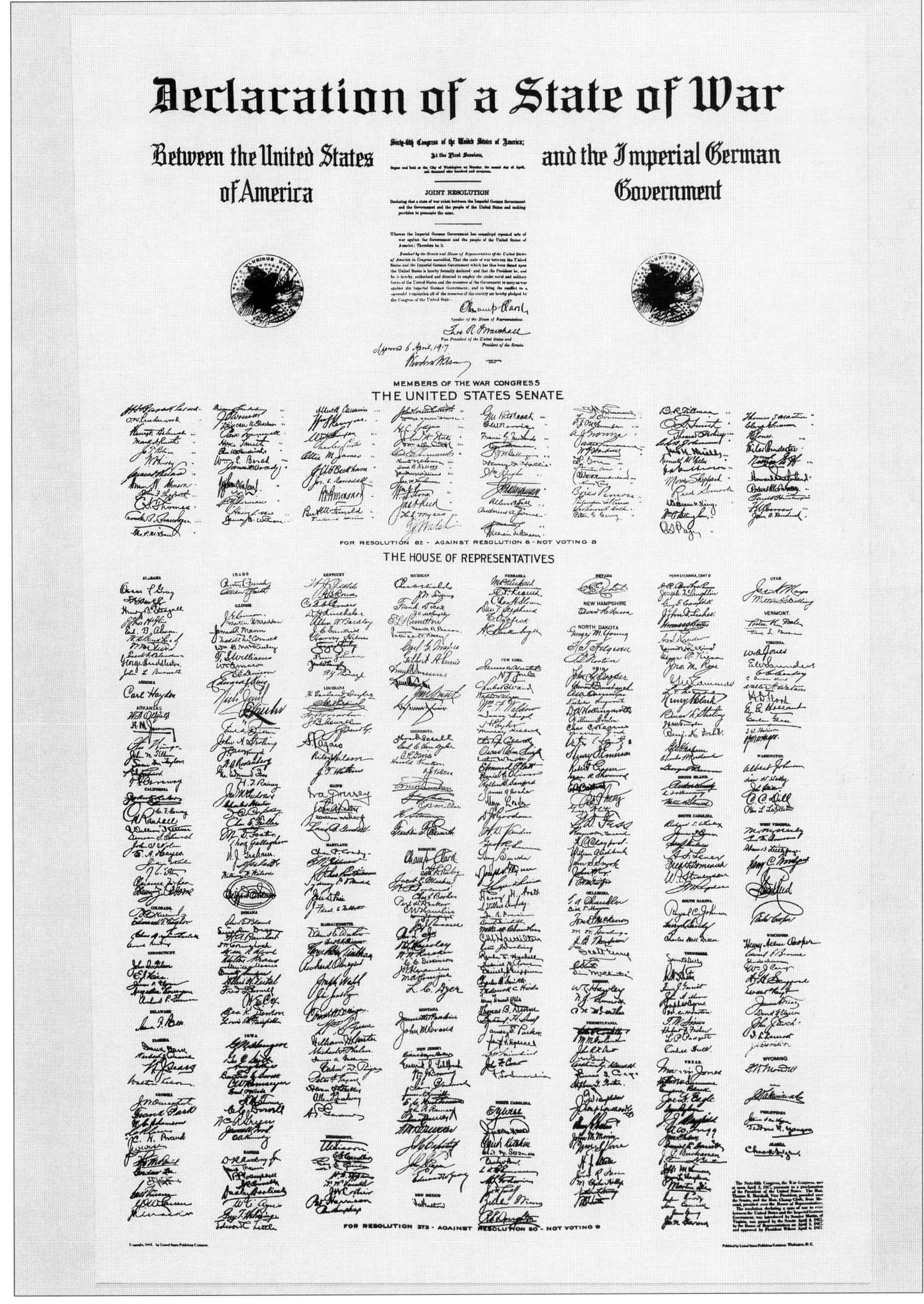

Declaration of a State of War

Between the United States of America and the Imperial German Government

Sixty-fifth Congress of the United States of America;
At the First Session,
Begun and held at the City of Washington on Monday, the second day of April, one thousand nine hundred and seventeen.

JOINT RESOLUTION

Declaring that a state of war exists between the Imperial German Government and the Government and the people of the United States and making provision to prosecute the same.

Whereas the Imperial German Government has committed repeated acts of war against the Government and the people of the United States of America: Therefore be it

Resolved by the Senate and House of Representatives of the United States of America in Congress assembled, That the state of war between the United States and the Imperial German Government which has thus been thrust upon the United States is hereby formally declared; and that the President be, and he is hereby, authorized and directed to employ the entire naval and military forces of the United States and the resources of the Government to carry on war against the Imperial German Government; and to bring the conflict to a successful termination all of the resources of the country are hereby pledged by the Congress of the United States.

Champ Clark
Speaker of the House of Representatives.

Thos. R. Marshall
Vice President of the United States and President of the Senate.

Approved 6 April, 1917
Woodrow Wilson

MEMBERS OF THE WAR CONGRESS

THE UNITED STATES SENATE

FOR RESOLUTION 82 - AGAINST RESOLUTION 6 - NOT VOTING 8

THE HOUSE OF REPRESENTATIVES

FOR RESOLUTION 373 - AGAINST RESOLUTION 50 - NOT VOTING 9

President Wilson asked Congress for a declaration of war on 2 April 1917. The Declaration of a State of War with the Imperial German Government passed the Senate by a vote of 86 to 6 and the House, 373 to 50, in the early morning of 6 April. (Courtesy National Archives.)

FOURTEEN POINTS

I. Open covenants of peace, openly arrived at, after which there shall be no private international understandings of any kind but diplomacy shall proceed always frankly and in the public view.

II. Absolute freedom of navigation upon the seas, outside territorial waters, alike in peace and war, except the seas may be closed in whole or in part by international action for the enforcement of international covenants.

III. The removal, so far as possible, of all economic barriers and the establishment of an equality of trade conditions among all the nations consenting to the peace and associating themselves for its maintenance.

IV. Adequate guarantees given and taken that national armaments will be reduced to the lowest point consistent with domestic safety.

V. A free, open-minded, and absolutely impartial adjustment of all colonial claims, based upon a strict observance of the principle that in determining all such questions of sovereignty the interests of the populations concerned must have equal weight with the equitable claims of the government whose title is to be determined.

VI. The evacuation of all Russian territory and such a settlement of all questions affecting Russia as will secure the best and freest cooperation of the other nations of the world in obtaining for her an unhampered and unembarrassed opportunity for the independent determination of her own political development and national policy and assure her of a sincere welcome into the society of free nations under institutions of her own choosing. . . .

VII. Belgium, the whole world will agree, must be evacuated and restored, without any attempt to limit the sovereignty which she enjoys in common with all other free nations. No other single act will serve as this will serve to restore confidence among the nations in the laws which they have themselves set. . . .

VIII. All French territory should be freed and the invaded portions restored, and the wrong done to France by Prussia in 1871 in the matter of Alsace-Lorraine, which has unsettled the peace of the world for nearly fifty years, should be righted, in order that peace may once more be made secure in the interest of all.

IX. A readjustment of the frontiers of Italy should be effected along clearly recognizable lines of nationality.

X. The peoples of Austria-Hungary, whose place among the nations we wish to see safeguarded and assured, should be accorded the freest opportunity of autonomous development.

XI. Rumania, Serbia, and Montenegro should be evacuated; occupied territories restored; Serbia accorded free and secure access to the sea; and the relations of the several Balkan states to one another determined by friendly counsel . . . ; and international guarantees of the political and economic independence and territorial integrity of the several Balkan states should be entered into.

XII. The Turkish portions of the present Ottoman Empire should be assured a secure sovereignty, but the other nationalities which are now under Turkish rule should be assured an undoubted security of life and an absolutely unmolested opportunity of autonomous development, and the Dardanelles should be permanently opened as a free passage to the ships and commerce of all nations under international guarantees.

XIII. An independent Polish state should be erected which should include the territories inhabited by indisputably Polish populations, which should be assured a free and secure access to the sea, and whose political and economic independence and territorial integrity should be guaranteed by international covenant.

XIV. A general association of nations must be formed under specific covenants for the purpose of affording mutual guarantees of political independence and territorial integrity to great and small states alike.

- *President Wilson presented his program for peace in a special message to Congress on 8 January 1918.*

WAR LEADER. Mobilizing the United States for war was a huge and complex process. Under Wilson's leadership the government virtually took over the U.S. economy, taking charge of the railroads, food production, industrial production, and labor relations. Wilson set up agencies to supervise these efforts and named qualified people to head them. He also met frequently with diplomats and military leaders from Great Britain and France, U.S. allies against Germany, about strategy in the war. U.S. troops began arriving in Europe in 1918. The demands of leadership put a heavy strain on Wilson's physical and mental health.

Wilson's greatest concern was the peace settlement with Germany after the war. Already, in January 1917, he had urged a "peace without victory" in which the German people would not be punished for the misdeeds of their leaders. After the U.S. entry into the war, he learned with dismay that Great Britain and France had previously signed secret treaties that would take away German territory and impose other heavy penalties. In reaction, in January 1918, Wilson declared that the United States would insist on certain provisions in a peace settlement with Germany. These "Fourteen Points" included a rejection of secret treaties and the for-

The Paris Peace Conference was dominated by the Big Four. Seated, left to right, are Premier Vittorio Orlando of Italy, Prime Minister David Lloyd George of Great Britain, Premier Georges Clemenceau of France, and President Woodrow Wilson. (Courtesy National Archives.)

President Wilson delivered a special message to Congress on 11 November 1918. First he read the terms of Germany's surrender, and then he discussed the end of the war that caused more than 300,000 U.S. casualties. (Courtesy National Archives.)

End of the War

. . . It is not now possible to assess the consequences of this great consummation. We know only that this tragical war, whose consuming flames swept from one nation to another until all the world was on fire, is at an end and that it was the privilege of our own people to enter it at its most critical juncture in such fashion and in such force as to contribute in a way of which we are all deeply proud to the great result. We know, too, that the object of the war is attained; the object upon which all free men had set their hearts; and attained with a sweeping completeness which even now we do not realize. Armed imperialism such as the men conceived who were but yesterday the masters of Germany is at an end, its illicit ambitions engulfed in black disaster. Who will now seek to revive it? The arbitrary power of the military caste of Germany which once could secretly and of its own single choice disturb the peace of the world is discredited and destroyed. And more than that,—much more than that,—has been accomplished. The great nations which associated themselves to destroy it have now definitely united in the common purpose to set up such a peace as will satisfy the longing of the whole world for disinterested justice, embodied in settlements which are based upon something much better and much more lasting than the selfish competitive interests of powerful states. There is no longer conjecture as to the objects the victors have in mind. They have a mind in the matter, not only, but a heart also. Their avowed and concerted purpose is to satisfy and protect the weak as well as to accord their just rights to the strong. . . .

- *Special message to Congress. 11 November 1918.*

mation of a new international organization, the League of Nations, to settle international disputes. He also took care to state publicly that the United States was acting independent of Great Britain and France and that it was their "associate," not their ally. He hinted that the United States might sign a separate treaty with Germany.

Before the congressional elections of 1918, Wilson asked the American people to give him a vote of confidence, as in a parliamentary system, by electing a Democratic majority. The results were a setback. Voters, tired of the war, returned a Republican majority in both houses. Wilson had to go into the postwar negotiations without assurance of congressional support, but he decided to proceed without asking the Republicans for advice.

THE TREATY OF VERSAILLES. The war ended 11 November 1918, when Germany agreed to an armistice. Wilson contributed greatly to securing the armistice. In letters, he assured the German Government that the final peace treaty would be based on the Fourteen Points and would be fair to Germany. In 1919, he traveled to Europe in person, a historic step for a U.S. president, to help draw up the peace treaties. No congressional leaders went with him. He met with the leaders of Great Britain, France, and Italy in France.

Wilson was hailed by enthusiastic European crowds and was awarded the Nobel Prize for peace, but he was less successful in bringing European leaders to his point of view. During the treaty negotiations, which lasted several months, Wilson was under great stress. Some historians have pointed out changes in his behavior and personality at this time as evidence that he was not a well man. The Treaty of Versailles, announced in June 1919, conformed only partly to Wilson's Fourteen Points. It was harshly punishing toward Germany. It imposed large payments and many restrictions, but it also provided, as Wilson wished, for the creation of a League of Nations.

Wilson returned to the United States in July 1919 to work for the adoption of the treaty, which had to be ratified by a two-thirds vote in the Senate. Getting Senate approval was difficult, because Senator Henry Cabot Lodge of Massachusetts, the leader of the Republican majority, despised Wilson personally and opposed the treaty. Lodge suggested changes in the treaty to protect U.S. sovereignty. Wilson stubbornly refused; he insisted that the treaty be passed just as it had been written at Versailles. When Lodge told him that the Senate

"On July 10, 1919, the President came before the Senate of the United States to present to it for its approval the treaty and the Covenant. Two of the Senators refused to stand up when he entered.

In the eyes of most of the men before him as he began to speak he was the schoolmaster incarnate raised to unthinkable heights from which he flung down not requests but dictates. In the most recent election, that of November 1918, days before the Armistice, he had asked the country to give him a Congress dominated by members of his own party. The request seemed unfair, partisan, to many voters; a Republican House and Senate were elected. But the President ignored the verdict and the implied suggestion that Republicans should have something to do with the peace and treaty-making and took no Republican of stature with him to Paris. Once there, he consulted only with himself. And in fact he had always been a self-contained thinker and planner, always treating politicians, even those of his own party (let alone the opposition) with suspicion. It was futile to spend much time with them, he said. No Senators were ever asked to a sociable lunch at the White House; their opinions were rarely requested under any circumstances. If given gratuitously, they were ignored."

• *Gene Smith,* When the Cheering Stopped: The Last Years of Woodrow Wilson.

Even sheet music was produced in support for the League of Nations. (Courtesy Collection of David J. and Janice L. Frent.)

would pass the treaty only if it contained certain changes in some of the articles, Wilson decided to go to the U.S. public. He planned a nationwide speaking tour to convince voters that the treaty should be passed without changes or reservations.

ILLNESS. Three weeks into his speaking tour, at Pueblo, Colorado, on 24 September, Wilson broke down during a speech. That night he woke with his left side paralyzed. He had had a massive stroke, but he still wanted to continue the tour. Mrs. Wilson ordered the train to return to Washington. (This was Wilson's second wife; his first had died in 1914. In 1915, he had married Edith Bolling Galt, the widow of a Washington jeweler.) In Washington, Wilson suffered another stroke. He was cared for in the White House by his personal staff. By Edith Wilson's orders, the seriousness of his condition was not revealed to the public or even to the vice president, Thomas R. Marshall of Indiana. Marshall was a homespun politician who had no desire for the presidency.

Wilson remained partially paralyzed for the rest of his term. The stroke also affected his vision. His mental abilities varied: at some times he was as articulate and rational as ever, and at others he had difficulty understanding or paying attention. He was subject to fits of temper or weeping. None of this was announced to the public. Only Edith Wilson and the President's doctor, Cary Grayson, knew the extent of his illness. Rumors circulated that Wilson was seriously ill, but on the few occasions when he met with senators or the cabinet, he appeared fit.

Wilson himself refused to acknowledge that he was ill. Although unable to leave the White House, he followed closely the Senate's consideration of the Versailles Treaty. Lodge had become the new chairman of the Senate Foreign Relations Committee. His advisers and his wife begged him to consent to some reservations so that the treaty would pass, but he refused. As a result, the Senate failed to ratify.

As for other government matters, Edith Wilson simply prevented many issues from reaching the President. To lighten his workload, she referred most problems to other government officials. Wilson did intervene in 1920 to prevent war with Mexico, which seemed imminent because of another crisis with the Carranza government. But he was not involved, for instance, in the raids against U.S. radicals carried out in 1919–1920 by his attorney general, A. Mitchell Palmer.

During the last years of Wilson's term, Congress passed two major amendments to the Constitution. Wilson was not deeply involved with either one. The Eighteenth (Prohibition) Amendment outlawed the sale, transportation, and manufacture of alcohol in the United States. Wilson opposed the Volstead Act which Congress passed to implement Prohibition, but Congress passed it over his veto. The Nineteenth Amendment extended voting rights to women.

ELECTION OF 1920. Wilson unrealistically felt that the Democrats should nominate him for a third term in 1920. Dr. Grayson lacked the courage to tell him how sick he really was. A few Democratic Party leaders, however, knew that Wilson was too ill to run, and they kept his name from being presented at the nominating convention. To Wilson's intense disappointment, the nominee was Governor James Cox of Ohio. Nevertheless, Wilson was confident that Cox would win, because he believed that U.S. voters supported the Versailles Treaty as strongly as he did. The election proved how wrong he was. Cox's Republican opponent, Senator Warren G. Harding, won overwhelmingly.

LAST YEARS. In failing health, Wilson retired to a town house on S Street in Washington. He intended to practice law but never recovered enough from his illness to do so effectively. Respected by the public for his many accomplishments, he died in Washington on 3 February 1924. He was buried in the Washington National Cathedral.

In the Senate it was voted that all business, including all committee meetings and investigations—which included the one concerning Teapot Dome—be suspended for three days. A delegation of Senators was appointed to attend the funeral. The Senate adjourned.

One of the Senators named as a member of the funeral delegation did not get home to his residence at 1765 Massachusetts Avenue, N.W., until several hours after the adjournment. He found waiting for him a note delivered by a Postal Telegraph boy. On the envelope was attached a Postal Telegraph sticker requesting an immediate reply. The note was handwritten. It said:

My Dear Sir:

I note in the papers that you have been designated by the Senate of the U.S. as one of those to attend Mr. Wilson's funeral.

As the funeral is private and not official and realizing that your presence would be embarrassing to you and unwelcome to me I write to request that you do not attend.

Yours truly,
Edith Bolling Wilson

The Senator wrote back in his own hand:

My Dear Madam:

I have just received your note, in which you say that the funeral services of Mr. Wilson are to be private and not official and that my presence would be unwelcome to you. When the Senate Committee was appointed I had no idea that the Committee was expected to attend the private services at the home and I had supposed that the services at the church were to be public.

You may rest assured that nothing could be more distasteful to me than to do anything which by any possibility could be embarrassing to you.

I have the honor to be

Very truly yours,
H.C. Lodge

• *From Gene Smith,* When the Cheering Stopped: The Last Years of Woodrow Wilson. *Senator Henry Cabot Lodge was a bitter enemy of President Wilson. He opposed the Versailles Treaty and led the fight against its ratification.*

VICE PRESIDENT

Thomas Riley Marshall
(1854–1925)

CHRONOLOGICAL EVENTS

1854	Born, North Manchester, Indiana, 14 March
1873	Graduated from Wabash College, Indiana
1908	Elected governor of Indiana
1912	Elected vice president
1925	Died, Washington, D.C., 1 June

BIOGRAPHY

A friendly, story-telling Hoosier, Thomas Riley Marshall was the son of a country doctor. As a child he wanted so much to become a lawyer that he spent much time in court listening to cases. After attending Wabash College and reading law, he opened his own practice. A bachelor who lived with his mother until he was past 40, he eventually married Lois Kimsey, a deputy county clerk.

Marshall lost his first race, for prosecuting attorney, in 1880. Although he served for many years in the Democratic state committee, he did not attempt another race until 1908, when he was elected governor of Indiana, a post that the Republicans had long held.

Indiana's Democratic boss, Tom Taggart, went to the Democratic convention in 1912 determined to nominate Marshall for vice president. Despite Taggart's dislike for the reform governor of New Jersey, Woodrow Wilson, he gave Indiana's delegates to Wilson in return for Marshall's selection for the second spot. The intellectual Wilson regarded Marshall as a "small-caliber man" whom he never took seriously. Although Wilson invited the Vice President to attend cabinet meetings, Marshall felt out of place and stopped going after one session. He similarly discovered that presiding over Senate sessions offered him little authority.

By contrast, Marshall received extensive press attention for his unassuming appearance and his love of telling folksy stories. He became a popular after-dinner speaker and lecturer. His most repeated line was, "What this country needs is a good five-cent cigar."

Although the President rarely consulted him, Marshall loyally supported Wilson's programs on Capitol Hill, and in 1916, he was renominated for another term. In 1919, Wilson went to France to negotiate the Treaty of Versailles and asked Marshall to preside over cabinet meetings in his absence. Arguing that he was more a part of the legislative than of the executive branch, Marshall gave up presiding after a brief time. Later that year, Wilson suffered a crippling stroke while speaking in behalf of the treaty. Although aware of the seriousness of Wilson's illness, Marshall refused to take any action that might appear to take over presidential responsibilities. Since Marshall would not preside over the cabinet, Secretary of State Robert Lansing called cabinet meetings, instead. Wilson later fired Lansing for insubordination.

Democrats ignored Marshall in choosing a presidential candidate in 1920. He retired to Indiana to write a witty memoir.

The Cabinet

Secretary of State
William Jennings Bryan, 1913
Robert Lansing, 1915, 1917
Bainbridge Colby, 1920

Secretary of War
Lindley M. Garrison, 1913
Newton D. Baker, 1916, 1917

Secretary of the Treasury
William Gibbs McAdoo, 1913, 1917
Carter Glass, 1918
David F. Houston, 1920

Postmaster General
Albert S. Burleson, 1913, 1917

Attorney General
James C. McReynolds, 1913
Thomas Watt Gregory, 1914, 1917
A. Mitchell Palmer, 1919

Secretary of the Navy
Josephus Daniels, 1913, 1917

Secretary of the Interior
Franklin K. Lane, 1913, 1917
John Barton Payne, 1920

Secretary of Agriculture
David F. Houston, 1913
Edwin T. Meredith, 1920

Secretary of Commerce[1]
William C. Redfield, 1913
Joshua W. Alexander, 1919

Secretary of Labor[1]
William B. Wilson, 1913, 1917

1. Department of Commerce and Labor established 14 February 1903; on 4 March 1913 divided into separate departments. The secretary of each was made a cabinet member.

(Courtesy National Archives.)

Josephus Daniels (1862–1948). Daniels was appointed secretary of the navy by President Woodrow Wilson in 1913.

Daniels was a notable journalist whose career encompassed politics and diplomacy. Becoming editor and publisher first of the *State Chronicle* (1895) and then of the *News and Observer* (1894) in Raleigh, North Carolina, he championed such causes as prohibition, women's rights, and public education.

As secretary of the navy, Daniels was criticized for inadequately preparing the U.S. Navy for World War I. Under President Franklin D. Roosevelt, he served as ambassador to Mexico (1933–1941).

He retired to Raleigh, North Carolina in 1941. He wrote *Our Navy at War* (1922), *Life of Woodrow Wilson* (1924), and *The Wilson Era* (1944–1946).

President Woodrow Wilson and his cabinet. Seated at the head of the table, on the left, President Wilson. Front row, left to right, Secretary of State Bainbridge Colby; Secretary of War Newton D. Baker; Postmaster General Albert S. Burleson; Secretary of the Interior John Barton Payne; and Secretary of Commerce Joshua W. Alexander. Back row, left to right, Secretary of the Treasury David F. Houston; Attorney General A. Mitchell Palmer; Secretary of the Navy Josephus Daniels; Secretary of Agriculture Edwin T. Meredith; and Secretary of Labor William B. Wilson.

This photograph was taken prior to the cabinet meeting of 15 February 1921 and is the last official photograph of Wilson and his cabinet. (Courtesy Library of Congress.)

FAMILY

CHRONOLOGICAL EVENTS

15 May 1860	Ellen Louise Axson born
15 October 1872	Edith Bolling born
24 June 1885	Ellen Axson married Woodrow Wilson
16 April 1886	Daughter, Margaret, born
28 August 1887	Daughter, Jessie, born
5 October 1889	Daughter, Eleanor, born
1896	Edith Bolling married Norman Galt
1908	Norman Galt died
6 August 1914	Ellen Wilson died
18 December 1915	Edith Bolling Galt married Woodrow Wilson
3 February 1924	Woodrow Wilson died
28 December 1961	Edith Bolling Galt Wilson died

Before Edith Wilson became ill in 1914, she oversaw the weddings of two of her daughters: Jessie and Eleanor. Jessie married Francis B. Sayre, who later joined the faculty at Harvard Law School. Eleanor fell in love with William Gibbs McAdoo, her father's secretary of the treasury. He was much older and a widower with grown children. They were married on 7 May 1914. Mrs. Wilson died two months later. She was very interested in slum clearance and providing better housing for African Americans in Washington. Before her death, Congress passed the legislation regarding slum clearance which she had endorsed.

President Woodrow Wilson was photographed with his first wife, Ellen, and their three daughters in 1912, the year he was elected. Edith Wilson was an accomplished artist, and she built a small studio for herself in the White House. (Courtesy Library of Congress.)

◀ Margaret Wilson studied voice and piano. During World War I, she sang at army camps and gave many concerts for the Red Cross. After she finally got her father's approval, she sang for the troops in France.

She moved to New York after her father's death and became very interested in Indian philosophy. She moved to India in 1939, and she died there in 1944.

(Courtesy Library of Congress.)

Edith Bolling Galt became engaged to President Wilson less than one year after his wife's death. They were married in a small ceremony at her home in Washington.

After the President suffered a stroke in 1919, she decided what material he should see and who should be allowed to visit him. She was accused of being "the first woman President." Whether this was true or not, it showed the seriousness of presidential disability.

She took care of her husband in their home in Washington until his death in 1924. She lived to attend President Kennedy's Inauguration in 1961, and died later that year. ▶

(Courtesy Library of Congress.)

The Woodrow Wilson Birthplace & Museum

P.O. Box 24
Staunton, Virginia 24402-0024
Tel: (703) 885-0897

The house in which Woodrow Wilson was born was built in 1846 by the Staunton Presbyterian Church as a home for its minister.
(Courtesy Library of Congress.)

Located at 18-24 North Coalter Street (Woodrow Wilson Parkway), across from Mary Baldwin College. Can be reached via I-81, Exit 58/225. Open daily from 9 A.M. to 5 P.M.; Sundays in January and February from 1 P.M. to 5 P.M. Closed Thanksgiving, Christmas, and New Year's Day. Admission fee, with discounts available for senior citizens. Special rates available for groups of 10 or more by advance reservation. Children ages 5 and under admitted free. First floor and basement level are handicapped accessible. Educational programs available for schoolchildren. Administered by the Woodrow Wilson Birthplace Foundation.

Woodrow Wilson was born on 28 December 1856 in a three-story brick home owned by the local Presbyterian church where his father, Rev. Dr. Joseph Ruggles Wilson, was a minister. The Wilson family lived there from March 1855 until November 1857, when Wilson's father was called to be the pastor of the First Presbyterian Church of Augusta, Georgia.

The birthplace home is furnished with Wilson family artifacts, photographs, and personal possessions. Included are the family Bible that records President Wilson's birth, musical instruments used by the family, portraits of Wilson's parents, and Wilson's letters and books. Period furniture similar to that used by the Wilson family are also part of the collection.

In 1990, a 13,000-square-foot mansion across from the reception house was renovated and then opened as the museum. It contains seven exhibit galleries that chart Wilson's life and times, a library, and rooms for school programs.

THE WOODROW WILSON HOUSE MUSEUM

2340 S Street, NW • Washington, D.C. 20008 • Tel: (202) 387-4062

Located at Massachusetts Avenue and S Street. Can be reached via Dupont Circle Metro. Open January through December, Tuesday to Sunday, from 10 A.M. to 4 P.M. Closed Thanksgiving, Christmas, and New Year's Day. Admission fee. Groups admitted year-round by reservation. Tours available. Handicapped accessible. Gift shop. Administered by the National Trust for Historic Preservation.

In 1920, President Wilson purchased a five-story, red brick town house in the Embassy Row section of Washington, D.C. as a surprise for his second wife, Edith Bolling Galt. Ten of Wilson's friends contributed to the purchase of the home, which was designed by architect Waddy B. Wood in 1915 for the Henry Parker Fairbanks family. The Wilsons made several renovations, including the addition of a two-car garage, a billiard room, book stacks for the President's 8,000-volume library, and an elevator. Wilson lived there until his death on 3 February 1924.

After Wilson's death, his widow, Edith, continued to live in the house, preserving its mementos and furnishings. Upon her death in 1961, her will gave the house and its contents to the National Trust for Historic Preservation.

▲ *Upon moving into their new home, Woodrow Wilson presented his wife, Edith, with a small piece of sod from the garden and the key to the front door—a Scottish tradition. He is the only president who chose to live in Washington, D.C. after leaving office.* (Courtesy Library of Congress.)

◀ *Woodrow Wilson died on 3 February 1924 at his home in Washington, D.C. The funeral was held at the Bethlehem Chapel of the Washington Cathedral, where he was buried. He is the only president buried in Washington, D.C.* (Courtesy Library of Congress.)

Warren G. Harding

CHRONOLOGICAL EVENTS

2 November 1865	Born, Corsica (now Blooming Grove), Ohio
1882	Graduated from Ohio Central College, Iberia, Ohio
November 1885	Became editor and proprietor of the *Marion Star*, Ohio
November 1899	Elected to Ohio State Senate
November 1901	Reelected to Ohio State Senate
November 1903	Elected lieutenant governor of Ohio
8 November 1910	Defeated for election as governor of Ohio
3 November 1914	Elected to U.S. Senate
2 November 1920	Elected president
4 March 1921	Inaugurated president
27 May 1921	Signed Emergency Tariff Act
10 June 1921	Signed act establishing the Bureau of the Budget in the Treasury Department
2 July 1921	Signed joint resolution ending the war with Germany
November 1921–February 1922	Washington Conference for the Limitation of Armament; Four-Power Treaty signed 13 December 1921
6 February 1922	Five-Power Treaty signed; Nine-Power Treaty signed
21 September 1922	Signed Fordney-McCumber Tariff Act
February 1923	Recommended U.S. join International Court of Justice
20 June 1923	Began transcontinental speaking tour
2 August 1923	Died, San Francisco, California

BIOGRAPHY

Warren G. Harding's brief administration—two years and five months—is remembered today mainly for the misdeeds of some of the officials who were a part of it rather than the few real achievements that were attained. Harding himself had little to do with either the misdeeds or the achievements. A likable, kindly man without unusual intelligence or talent, he rose to the presidency because of the ambition of the people around him. In policy matters he relied on his subordinates, preferring to concentrate on his ceremonial duties.

EARLY LIFE. Harding was born 2 November 1865 in Corsica, Ohio, the oldest son of George Tryon Harding, a country doctor, and Phoebe Dickerson Harding, a midwife. He grew up in the village of Caledonia, Ohio, developing into a tall, strong, and handsome man. Harding was a confident speaker and popular with his peers during his two years at Ohio Central College, a small rural academy, where he played in the band and edited the student newspaper. His formal education ended when he was 16 years old.

NEWSPAPERMAN. At age 16, Harding moved to the larger town of Marion, Ohio, where his father had set up a medical practice. There, Harding tried various fields, including teaching and selling insurance. In 1884, he and two friends purchased a struggling independent newspaper, the *Marion Star,* for a small amount of money, and Harding took over as editor. Within four years, his friendliness and his sales ability made the *Star* the leading newspaper in the county. In 1891, Harding married Florence Kling De Wolfe, a possessive, ambitious woman several years older than he. Mrs. Harding supervised the finances and operations of the newspaper, leaving Harding time for his other interest, the Republican Party.

POLITICIAN. Because of his fine voice and his good looks, Harding was soon in great demand as a Republican speaker. He enjoyed the company of politicians and decided to seek public office himself. In 1899, he was elected state senator, and he served two terms, making enough friends to win the nomination for lieutenant governor. Elected to that office in 1903, he served one term and hoped to be nominated for governor, but the state convention passed him over, and he returned in 1905 to Marion and the *Star*. By then, he was well known throughout the state. Harding, however, had little impact on public policy in any of these positions. He stood for no particular interest or program. He did, however, make many friends, especially Harry M. Daugherty, a lobbyist from Fayette County who thought of him as a potential president.

In 1914, Ohio Republicans, weary of internal battles between supporters of former President Theodore Roosevelt and those of former President William Howard Taft, needed a U.S. Senate candidate who would be inoffensive to both factions. They chose Harding, who was elected. His six years in the Senate, like his six years in Ohio politics, were

Inaugural Address

. . . We are ready to associate ourselves with the nations of the world great and small, for conference, for counsel; to seek the expressed views of world opinion; to recommend a way to approximate disarmament and relieve the crushing burdens of military and naval establishments. We elect to participate in suggesting plans for mediation, conciliation, and arbitration, and would gladly join in that expressed conscience of progress, which seeks to clarify and write the laws of international relationship, and establish a world court for the disposition of such justiciable questions as nations are agreed to submit thereto. In expressing aspirations, in seeking practical plans, in translating humanity's new concept of righteousness and justice and its hatred of war into recommended action we are ready most heartily to unite, but every commitment must be made in the exercise of our national sovereignty. Since freedom impelled, and independence inspired, and nationality exalted, a world supergovernment is contrary to everything we cherish and can have no sanction by our Republic. This is not selfishness, it is sanctity. It is not aloofness, it is security. It is not suspicion of others, it is patriotic adherence to the things which made us what we are. . . .

- *The biggest issue in the election of 1920 was the League of Nations. The Democrats wanted the United States to join it. The Republicans said that they would support some kind of international peacekeeping organization but not one that would not allow the United States to act as it wished.*

Warren G. Harding was sworn in as president on 4 March 1921. Chief Justice Edward D. White administered the oath. The Republican convention in Chicago, Illinois was apparently deadlocked after nine ballots. General Leonard Wood, former army chief of staff; Governor Frank Lowden of Illinois; and Senator Hiram Johnson of California were all running ahead of Harding. Republican Party leaders met that night in a room at the Blackstone Hotel—the "smoke-filled room"—and chose Harding. Harding received the nomination on the 10th ballot the next day. (Courtesy National Archives.)

unimpressive. He made friends and enjoyed life in Washington, but he took no leadership role and was frequently absent from Senate votes. Although he was keynote speaker at the 1916 Republican National Convention, his two-hour speech failed to stir the audience.

THE 1920 ELECTION. The presidential election of 1920 took place at an exciting time. World War I had just ended, and the United States was deeply divided over whether to join the League of Nations, an organization designed to preserve world peace. The Democratic president, Woodrow Wilson, had been very ill for months; the national economy was in turmoil as industry readjusted to peacetime; national prohibition of alcohol was about to go into effect; and women had just received the right to vote in all elections.

PRESIDENT. Harding brought the relaxed atmosphere of small-town business to the White House. He enjoyed personally greeting tourists to

President and Mrs. Harding were driven to the White House after the Inauguration ceremonies. He had received 60 percent of the popular vote and easily defeated the Democratic candidate, James M. Cox, who received 34 percent of the vote. The Socialist candidate, Eugene V. Debs, received 3 percent of the popular vote and the Farmer-Labor candidate, P.P. Christensen, received 1 percent. (Courtesy National Archives.)

the official residence. He spent two afternoons a week golfing and three evenings a week playing poker. Although the sale and transportation of alcoholic beverages were prohibited by federal law, he had whiskey in the White House for himself and visitors.

In policy matters, Harding deferred to his cabinet. Most of his major appointments were excellent: Charles Evans Hughes as secretary of state; Andrew Mellon as secretary of the treasury; and future president Herbert Hoover as secretary of commerce. Under Hughes's guidance, the United States took the lead in trying to avoid another global conflict like World War I, sponsoring the Washington Conference on the limitation of weapons. This conference in 1922 produced the Treaty of Washington, in which the leading nations agreed to restrictions on the size of their navies. Harding opposed U.S. entry into the League of Nations, but he did favor U.S. participation in the International Court of Justice set up by the League.

In domestic affairs, Treasury Secretary Mellon felt it was important to bring federal spending, which had grown immensely during World War I,

Warren G. Harding made the first official visit of a United States President to Canada. He spoke at Vancouver, British Columbia just prior to becoming ill. (Courtesy Library of Congress.)

THE RIGHTS OF BLACK CITIZENS

. . . I would insist upon equal educational opportunity for both (black and white races). This does not mean that both would become equally educated within a generation or two generations or ten generations. Even men of the same race do not accomplish such an equality as that. There must be such education among the colored people as will enable them to develop their own leaders capable of understanding and sympathizing with such a differentiation between the races as I have suggested—leaders who will inspire the race with proper ideals of race pride, of national pride, of an honorable destiny; and important participation in the universal effort for advancement of humanity as a whole. Racial amalgamation there cannot be. Partnership of the races in developing the highest aims to all humanity there must be if humanity, not only here but everywhere, is to achieve the ends which we have set for it.

I can say to you people of the South, both white and black, that the time has passed when you are entitled to assume that this problem of races is peculiarly and particularly your problem. More and more it is becoming a problem of the North; more and more it is the problem of Africa, of South America, of the Pacific of the South Seas, of the world. It is the problem of democracy everywhere, if we mean the things we say about democracy as the ideal political state. . . .

• *President Harding surprised his audience in Birmingham, Alabama on 26 October 1921. He called for educational, political, and economic equality between the races. The Democrats had attacked Harding for his beliefs in equal rights and had accused him of having "black blood."*

President Harding's sudden death in San Francisco, California shocked and saddened the country. His funeral was held in Washington, D.C. and his body was then returned to Marion, Ohio. (Courtesy Library of Congress.)

under control. At his suggestion, Congress in 1921 created the Bureau of the Budget to coordinate spending and removed the heaviest wartime taxes. Congress also passed the Emergency Tariff Act of 1921 and the Fordney-McCumber Tariff Act of 1922 to protect U.S. producers from foreign competition.

Harding appointed friends from Ohio and from the U.S. Senate to other offices. Harry M. Daugherty, for example, became attorney general. Many turned out to be incompetent or corrupt. Notably corrupt were Charles Forbes in the Veterans' Bureau and Secretary of the Interior Albert Fall. The best-known scandal of the Harding presidency, the leasing of the Teapot Dome oil reserve, took place in Fall's department. By 1923, evidence of their misconduct had come to Harding's attention. He fired Forbes and began an investigation into his activities. His friends' betrayal disturbed him greatly, and the worry aggravated a preexisting heart condition. Returning from an official trip to Alaska in August 1923, he died of a heart attack in San Francisco.

VICE PRESIDENT

Calvin Coolidge (1872–1933)

CHRONOLOGICAL EVENTS

1872	Born, Plymouth, Vermont, 4 July
1895	Graduated from Amherst College, Vermont
1898	Elected to Northampton City Council
1906	Elected to Massachusetts State House of Representatives
1911	Elected to Massachusetts State Senate
1918	Elected governor of Massachusetts
1920	Elected vice president
1923	Became president upon the death of Warren G. Harding
1924	Elected president
1933	Died, Northampton, Massachusetts, 5 January

BIOGRAPHY

Calvin Coolidge's mother died when he was a boy, so he was raised by his father, who ran a general store, farmed, and dabbled in politics in Vermont. Coolidge liked school much more than farm work. He attended Black River Academy and Amherst College. Then he joined a law firm in Northampton, Massachusetts. Elected to the Northampton City Council in 1898, he later became city solicitor. He served in both houses of the Massachusetts legislature, becoming president of the state senate. Firmly conservative, he viewed most reforms as harmful for business and believed it more important to kill bad bills than to pass good ones.

After the progressives left the Republican Party in 1912, conservatives took firm control of the state organization. Coolidge was elected lieutenant governor in 1914 and governor in 1918. In 1919, Boston's overworked and underpaid police went on strike. Governor Coolidge gave support to the police commissioner who refused to rehire the strikers. Coolidge's statement that "There is no right to strike against the public safety by anybody, anywhere, any time" won him enormous public acclaim.

In 1920, the Republicans chose the conservative Senator Warren G. Harding of Ohio to run for president. Party leaders wanted to nominate a progressive senator for vice president to balance the ticket, but a delegate proposed Coolidge from the floor. Spontaneously and enthusiastically, the convention nominated him. Harding and Coolidge won in a landslide.

Naturally shy and silent, Coolidge enjoyed the sedate responsibilities of presiding over the U.S. Senate. He conducted himself impassively and exerted little influence over the legislative or executive branches. President Harding invited him to cabinet meetings, but he never said a word at them. Many expected Coolidge to be dropped from the ticket in the 1924 election.

Scandal shook the Harding administration in 1923 when the Senate investigated illegal leasing of oil from federal lands at Teapot Dome, Wyoming. While traveling on the West Coast that August, a depressed President Harding died suddenly. Vacationing in Vermont, Coolidge took the oath as president from his father, a justice of the peace.

THE CABINET

SECRETARY OF STATE
Charles Evans Hughes, 1921

SECRETARY OF WAR
John W. Weeks, 1921

SECRETARY OF THE TREASURY
Andrew W. Mellon, 1921

POSTMASTER GENERAL
Will H. Hays, 1921
Hubert Work, 1922
Harry S. New, 1923

ATTORNEY GENERAL
Harry M. Daugherty, 1921

SECRETARY OF THE NAVY
Edwin Denby, 1921

SECRETARY OF THE INTERIOR
Albert B. Fall, 1921
Hubert Work, 1923

SECRETARY OF AGRICULTURE
Henry C. Wallace, 1921

SECRETARY OF COMMERCE
Herbert C. Hoover, 1921

SECRETARY OF LABOR
James J. Davis, 1921

John W. Weeks is shown here with President Harding (left) and Brigadier General Douglas MacArthur (right) reviewing the cadets of the U.S. Military Academy at West Point. (Courtesy Library of Congress.)

John W. Weeks (1860–1926). Weeks was appointed secretary of war by President Warren G. Harding in 1921. He had previously served in the U.S. Senate (1913–1919). After the death of President Harding, he retained his post in the administration of Calvin Coolidge.

As secretary of war, Weeks supervised the final transition from a wartime to a peacetime military. He established the Army Industrial College at Fort McNair. Weeks disagreed with General William "Billy" Mitchell's assessment of aviation in national defense.

Davis (right) is shown here with President Herbert C. Hoover in 1929. (Courtesy Herbert Hoover Presidential Library-Museum.)

James J. Davis (1873–1947). Davis served as secretary of labor under Presidents Harding, Coolidge, and Hoover (1921–1930).

Davis was a Welsh immigrant and a former tin mill worker. Most of his life, however, was devoted to the Loyal Order of the Moose. As director general for many years, he organized hundreds of new lodges.

A stocky, robust man, hearty and outgoing, "Puddler Jim" believed in the American dream, with its virtues of hard work and self-help. As labor secretary, he viewed trade unions more as benevolent associations than as opponents of capital and felt that strikes were seldom justified.

FAMILY

CHRONOLOGICAL EVENTS

15 August 1860	Florence (Flossie) Mabel Kling born	8 July 1891	Florence Kling married Warren G. Harding
1880	Florence Kling married Henry DeWolfe	2 August 1923	Warren G. Harding died
1886	Florence Kling divorced Henry DeWolfe	21 November 1924	Florence Harding died

When Florence Kling was 19 years old, she eloped with a neighbor, Henry DeWolfe. He later deserted her. She was left with a son who was raised by her parents. She divorced DeWolfe and married Warren G. Harding, when she was 30 years old. She helped her husband build his newspaper, the *Marion Star,* into a financial success, but their marriage was not a happy one. She was a demanding and headstrong woman. Her husband neglected her and had at least two affairs. She was with him in San Francisco when he died. Fifteen months later, Mrs. Harding died in Marion, Ohio, where she was born.

(Courtesy Ohio Historical Society.)

PLACES

HARDING HOME AND MUSEUM

380 Mount Vernon Avenue • Marion, Ohio 43302 • Tel: (614) 387-9630

Located on State Route 95, approximately 43 miles north of Columbus. Open Memorial Day through Labor Day, Wednesday to Saturday, from 9:30 A.M. to 5 P.M.; Sunday from 12 P.M. to 5 P.M. Labor Day through October, Saturday from 9:30 A.M. to 5 P.M.; Sunday from 12 P.M. to 5 P.M. November through May, Monday to Friday, open by appointment only. Admission fee, with discounts available for senior citizens and children ages 12 and under. Special rates available by arrangement for tour and school groups. Administered by the Ohio Historical Society.

Warren G. Harding and his wife, Florence, built the home in 1891. They lived there until his election to the presidency in 1920. The two-story house where Harding conducted his famous "front porch campaign" was restored to its turn-of-the-century appearance between 1964 and 1965. The original gaslights were restored, period decorations were duplicated in detail, and the original furnishings were returned.

The Harding Memorial is located south of Marion on State Route 423. The circular monument of white marble is situated within a 10-acre landscaped park. The Harding Memorial Association was formed in October 1923. In 1925, the design by Henry F. Hornbostel and Eric Fisher Wood was chosen for the memorial. Construction began in April 1926. The cornerstone, which contained a small collection of records and souvenirs, was laid by Vice President Charles G. Dawes on 30 May 1926. One year later, the bodies of President Harding and his wife, Florence, were moved to the Memorial.

▲ *The Press Building, located at the rear of the house, was built in 1920 as the headquarters for reporters during Harding's presidential campaign. It was transformed into a museum.* (Courtesy Ohio Historical Society.)

The Harding Memorial Association raised almost 1 million dollars for the construction of the memorial. Contributors included approximately 200,000 schoolchildren who donated pennies to the fund. (Courtesy Ohio Historical Society.) ▶

Calvin Coolidge

30TH PRESIDENT

OF THE UNITED STATES OF AMERICA

CHRONOLOGICAL EVENTS

4 July 1872	Born, Plymouth Notch, Vermont
26 June 1895	Graduated from Amherst College, Massachusetts
1897	Admitted to bar, Northampton, Massachusetts
1898	Elected to city council, Northampton, Massachusetts
1906	Elected to Massachusetts State House of Representatives
1909	Elected mayor of Northampton
1911	Elected to Massachusetts State Senate
1914	Elected president of Massachusetts State Senate
1915	Elected lieutenant governor of Massachusetts
November 1918	Elected governor of Massachusetts
September 1919	Boston Police Strike
November 1919	Reelected governor of Massachusetts
2 November 1920	Elected vice president
2 August 1923	Became president upon the death of Warren G. Harding
15 May 1924	Vetoed Veterans' Bonus Bill
19 May 1924	Veterans' Bonus Bill passed over his veto
26 May 1924	Signed Immigration Act (Johnson Bill)
4 November 1924	Elected president
4 March 1925	Inaugurated president
25 February 1927	Vetoed McNary-Haugen farm relief bill
2 August 1927	Announced that he would not run for reelection
27 August 1928	Kellogg-Briand Pact signed (also known as Pact of Paris)
21 December 1928	Signed Boulder Dam Act (renamed Hoover Dam)
1929	Published memoirs, *The Autobiography of Calvin Coolidge*
5 January 1933	Died, Northampton, Massachusetts

BIOGRAPHY

Calvin Coolidge was a rarity among U.S. presidents—an accidental president with few political allies who was, nevertheless, popular and respected during his term of office. Voters liked his honesty, thrift, and moderation. His successful efforts to make government cheaper and more efficient were, in the long run, overturned by the new social programs set up to combat the Great Depression. Likewise, his efforts to promote world peace were undermined by the coming of World War II.

EARLY LIFE. John Calvin Coolidge (he dropped his first name after graduating from college) was born on 4 July 1872, in Plymouth Notch, a tiny community deep in the hills of Vermont. His father,

Calvin Coolidge graduated from Amherst College in 1895. This is his senior portrait. (Courtesy Forbes Library.)

John, was a community leader, who farmed, sold insurance, lent money, and held various local political offices. His mother, Victoria, died when he was 12. Until he was 13, he was educated in a small stone schoolhouse up the hill from his home. He was a shy boy who liked reading and had no desire to become rich or important.

EDUCATION. At age 13, Coolidge entered Black River Academy in Ludlow, a village 12 miles from Plymouth Notch. He did well there and became interested in public speaking. His father decided he should attend college, and in September 1891, Coolidge entered Amherst College in Massachusetts. Because of his rural background and small-town education, he was lonely there and found the work difficult at first. His grades improved after two years and his classmates accepted him as a clever, witty speaker. He graduated in 1895.

LAWYER AND LOCAL POLITICIAN. Coolidge would have preferred to return home and keep the general store, but at his father's insistence he prepared to use his speaking skills by studying to be a lawyer. He began as a clerk in a law office in Northampton, Massachusetts, only a few miles from Amherst. After two years of concentrated study, he passed his bar examination and opened his own office. Success as a lawyer came slowly but steadily. At the same time, he became active in the local Republican Party, as his father had been active in Vermont. In 1898, Coolidge was elected to the Northampton city council. In the following years, he held a number of local offices. From 1910 to 1911, he served as mayor, cutting taxes and expanding city services. His honesty and economy made him popular with the voters.

STATE POLITICS. In 1905, Coolidge married Grace Goodhue, a Vermont-born teacher at the Clarke School for the Deaf. Two years later, he began seeking state political office—because, he said, the experience might improve his law practice. His pattern was the same as the one he had followed in local politics: a few terms in one office, followed by a move up to the next level. He served two years (1907–1908) in the Massachusetts State House of Representatives. After a six-year interval spent in local politics, he served four years (1912–1915) in the Massachusetts State Senate. He generally supported reform and progressive bills and became a popular candidate, always sure of reelection.

GOVERNOR. As Coolidge rose in politics, he attracted the attention of a number of Massachusetts businessmen, particularly Amherst graduates, who respected his talents and urged him to stay in office. With their support, he was elected lieutenant governor in 1915. Three years later, he was elected governor. He became governor just after World War I ended, at a time of economic instability. People feared poverty, unemployment, and disorder.

THE BOSTON POLICE STRIKE. Coolidge became nationally famous as governor because of his response to a local crisis. In September 1919, three quarters of the Boston police force walked off the job because the police commissioner refused to recognize their union. Governor Coolidge replaced them with the State Guard and supported the police commissioner in his refusal to rehire any of the striking policemen. Samuel Gompers of the American Federation of Labor insisted that the men were exercising their rights as workers. Coolidge replied, in a telegram to Gompers: "There is no right to strike against the public safety by anybody, anywhere, any time." That phrase, as Coolidge put it, "caught the attention of the nation." President Woodrow Wilson expressed his support for Coolidge's position. So did citizens from all over the country who were fearful of disorder and lawlessness. Coolidge had expected that his statement would cost him popularity and would lead to his defeat for reelection in November. Instead, he was reelected by 100,000 more votes than he had received the previous year.

THE 1920 CONVENTION. Enthusiastic Massachusetts Republicans at once began promoting Coolidge for the Republican nomination for president in 1920. Coolidge decided not to leave Massachusetts to campaign actively. He preferred to stay in the background so that he could be a compromise choice if the leading candidates deadlocked. At the national convention in Chicago, there was a deadlock, but Coolidge was not the final choice. An influential group of senators managed to get the nomination for their candidate, Senator Warren G. Harding of Ohio. Many convention delegates, however, were unhappy about Harding and continued to respect Coolidge. When his name was proposed for vice president, the convention abandoned the candidate of the party bosses and chose Coolidge for the second spot. In November, the Harding-Coolidge ticket won easily. The Democrat whom Coolidge defeated for the vice presidency was also a future president—Franklin D. Roosevelt.

VICE PRESIDENT. Coolidge found the vice presidency unsatisfying. Not being rich, he could not afford a house in Washington. He and his wife, Grace, lived in a suite of rooms at the New Willard Hotel. He had few political friends and did not make new ones easily. His main responsibility, presiding over the U.S. Senate, frustrated him because of the difficult personalities of the senators and the mystifying rules of the body. At Harding's request, he sat in on cabinet meetings and became well informed on policy matters, but he rarely expressed an opinion. Because of his silence and his rural New England ways, he began to develop a reputation in Washington as an odd character.

PRESIDENT. On 2 August 1923 President Harding, returning from a trip to Alaska, died in San Francisco of a massive stroke. Coolidge was vacationing at his father's home in Plymouth Notch, where there was no telephone. He was awakened after midnight by a crowd of newspaper reporters and Secret Service agents who had driven up the mountain with the news. Coolidge's father, a notary public, administered the oath of office in

Calvin Coolidge was not happy as President Warren G. Harding's vice president. He and Grace, his wife, are shown here (right) with the Hardings. (Courtesy Library of Congress.)

William Allen White wrote in his biography, President Coolidge: A Puritan in Babylon: *"He has lived and will die, no matter where fate sends him, Cal Coolidge, of Northampton, of Ludlow and of Plymouth, the small-town American who is more typical of America than our cosmopolitan boulevardier. . . . One flag, one conscience, one wife, and never more than three words will do him all his life."*

Mrs. Coolidge told the story of a hostess who opened her conversation at the dinner table with a challenge:

"You must talk to me, Mr. Coolidge, I made a bet today that I could get more than two words out of you."

"You lose," the President replied. (Courtesy Library of Congress)

John Calvin Coolidge administered the oath of office to his son at 2:47 A.M. *on 3 August 1923. When President Coolidge arrived in Washington, he was told that the oath was not valid because his father was not a federal judge.* (Courtesy Library of Congress.)

the front parlor of his boyhood home.

Coolidge was in an unusual position as he assumed the presidency. He had few allies in the Republican Party and none at all among Democrats. Essentially, he was an independent president. He portrayed himself as a caretaker, pledged to continue Harding's policies of tax reduction and international arms limitation, and asked the cabinet to remain. Most Washington political observers doubted that the Republicans would renominate him in 1924. However, the public reaction to him was unexpectedly favorable. People admired his simplicity, integrity, and absence of pretense. By the end of 1923, he seemed like the best candidate the Republicans could choose.

THE HARDING SCANDALS. Shortly after Coolidge took office, a Senate investigation began revealing evidence of corruption by Harding's appointees in the Veterans' Bureau and the Department of the Interior (the so-called "Teapot Dome" scandals). At first, Coolidge believed these revelations politically motivated. As the evidence of corruption piled up, he took action, dismissing the guilty employees. Senators found no indication that he was connected with the corrupt behavior. His actions in the White House made clear the difference between his administration and that of the sociable, easygoing Harding. Harding had gambled and consumed illegal liquor in the executive mansion. Under Coolidge the atmosphere in the White

House was dignified and rather cold, like that of "a New England front parlor," as Alice Roosevelt Longworth, the sharp-tongued daughter of Theodore Roosevelt, put it. The public approved of the change.

THE 1924 CAMPAIGN. Coolidge had no serious competition for the Republican nomination. A large group of progressives, however, favored more active government policy. They left the Republican Party to revive Theodore Roosevelt's old Progressive Party. They named Senator Robert LaFollette of Wisconsin as their presidential candidate. This Republican split might have hurt Coolidge's chance of reelection if there had been a strong Democratic nominee, but there was not. The Democratic Party, tormented by disagreements over social issues like nativism and Prohibition, chose John W. Davis. Davis was a Wall Street lawyer who had served competently in President Wilson's administration but was unknown to the public. In the election, Coolidge and his running mate, Charles G. Dawes, soundly defeated both LaFollette and Davis. For Coolidge, however, the later part of the campaign was overshadowed by the death in July of his teen-aged son. Calvin Jr. had gotten a blister while playing tennis on the White House courts. He died of the infection. "When he went, the power and the glory of the Presidency went with him," Coolidge wrote later.

DOMESTIC POLICY. Inaugurated in 1925, Coolidge was now president in his own right and free to develop his own policy. Its emphasis was economy in government. Coolidge could not stand waste. By tightening the government's expenditures in collaboration with Treasury Secretary Andrew Mellon, he was able to reduce its need for revenue. The Revenue Act of 1926, which reduced taxes by 10 percent, virtually eliminated taxes for most middle-class Americans. By 1929, the wealthiest citizens were paying 93 percent of federal taxes. This was in accordance with Coolidge's belief: "The wealth of our country is not public wealth, but private wealth. It does not belong to Government, it belongs to the people." At the same time, Coolidge's administration reduced the national debt by $2 billion in three years.

In other areas, he was less successful in dealing with the Republican Congress. An important area of disagreement was farm policy. Congress several times passed the McNary-Haugen farm bill which would have authorized the sale of surplus U.S. farm products to other countries through a government agency. Coolidge thought the idea too costly and complicated. He opposed the bill and vetoed it twice. He also opposed a bill to end Japanese immigration to the United States, but Congress overrode his veto. In speeches, Coolidge criticized discrimination and materialism in American life, but he proposed no government action against either.

Veto of the McNary-Haugen Bill

. . . Clearly this legislation involves government fixing of prices. It gives the proposed Federal board almost unlimited authority to fix prices on the designated commodities. This is price fixing, furthermore, on some of the Nation's basic foods and materials. Nothing is more certain than that such price fixing would upset the normal exchange relationships existing in the open market and that it would finally have to be extended to cover a multitude of other goods and services. Government price fixing, once started, has alike no justice and no end. It is an economic folly from which this country has every right to be spared. . . .

• *President Coolidge thought that the McNary-Haugen Bill was socialistic. He vetoed it in February 1927 and again in May 1928.*

INTERNATIONAL AFFAIRS. Coolidge's main aim in foreign policy, like Harding's, was to prevent a recurrence of the terrible conflict and slaughter of

The Kellogg-Briand Pact

. . . While it is incumbent upon us to secure such advantages as we can from our adversity, we all recognize that we should take every precaution to prevent ourselves or the rest of the world from being involved again in such a tragedy as began in 1914. While the country's national defense should never be neglected, preparation for the maintenance of peace is likewise required by every humane impulse that stirs the hearts of men. Those of you who have seen service would be the first to say that if the country needed you, you would respond again. But you will also be the first to say that you require of your government that it should take every possible precaution that human ingenuity can devise to insure the settlement of its differences with other countries through diplomatic negotiations and mutual concessions according to the dictates of reason, rather than by appeal to force.

It is in accordance with our determination to refrain from aggression and build up a sentiment and practice among nations more favorable to peace, that we ratified a treaty for the limitation of naval armaments made in 1921, earnestly sought for a further extension of this principle in 1927, and have secured the consent of fourteen important nations to the negotiation of a treaty condemning recourse to war, renouncing it is an instrument of national policy, and pledging each other to seek no solution of their disagreements except by pacific means. It is hoped other nations will join in this movement. Had an agreement of this kind been in existence in 1914, there is every reason to suppose that it would have saved the situation and delivered the world from all the misery which was inflicted by the great war.

By taking a leading position in security this agreement, which is fraught with so much hope for the progress of humanity, we have demonstrated that when we have said we maintained our armaments, not for aggression, but purely for defense, we were making a candid statement which we were willing to verify by our actions.

I shall not now go into a discussion of the details or the implications of this agreement other than to point out that, of course, it detracts nothing from the right and obligation of ourselves or the other high contracting parties to maintain an adequate national defense against any attack, but it does pledge ourselves not to attack others in consideration for their agreement not to attack us, and to seek a settlement of our controversies one with another through peaceful means.

While it would be too much to suppose that was has been entirely banished yet a new and important barrier, reasonable and honorable, has been set up to prevent it. This agreement proposes a revolutionary policy among nations. It holds a greater hope for peaceful relations than was ever before given to the world. If those who are involved in it, having started it will finish it, its provisions will prove one of the greatest blessings ever bestowed upon humanity. It is a fitting consummation of the first decade of peace.

- *The United States and 14 other nations signed the Kellogg-Briand Pact, also known as the Pact of Paris, in 1928. It pledged all signers—there were later 47 more nations—to renounce war "as an instrument of national policy in their relations with one another."*

President Coolidge spoke to the American Legion in Wausau, Wisconsin on 15 August 1928. He urged ratification of the pact even though he did not have much confidence in it. Congress ratified the Kellogg-Briand Pact in 1929.

AUTOBIOGRAPHY OF CALVIN COOLIDGE

. . . It is difficult for men in high office to avoid the malady of self-delusion. They are always surrounded by worshippers. They are constantly, and for the most part sincerely, assured of their greatness.

They live an artificial atmosphere of adulation and exaltation which sooner or later impairs their judgment. They are in grave danger of becoming careless and arrogant.

The chances of having wise and faithful public service are increased by a change in the Presidential office after a moderate length of time.

It is necessary for the head of the nation to differ with many people who are honest in their opinions. As his term progresses, the number who are disappointed accumulates. Finally, there is so large a body who have lost confidence in him that he meets a rising opposition which makes his efforts less effective.

In the higher ranges of public service men appear to come forward to perform a certain duty. When it is performed their work is done. They usually find it impossible to readjust themselves in the thought of the people so as to pass on successfully to the solution of new public problems.

An examination of the records of those Presidents who have served eight years will disclose that in almost every instance the latter part of their term has shown very little in the way of constructive accomplishment. They have often been clouded with grave disappointments.

While I had a desire to be relieved of the pretensions and delusions of public life, it was not because of any attraction of pleasure or idleness.

We draw our Presidents from the people. It is a wholesome thing for them to return to the people. I came from them. I wish to be one of them again. . . .

- *Coolidge explained his decision not to run for reelection in 1928 in his autobiography. He said, "I do not choose to run." He noted that George Washington had said almost the same thing in his Farewell Address, where he announced that "choice and prudence" invited him to retire.*

World War I—then known as "The Great War." By extending credit to European countries, especially Germany, the United States tried to keep them prosperous, stable, and not inclined to go to war. (Much of this policy was carried out by the Federal Reserve and was not under Coolidge's direct control. This contributed to the ballooning of credit in the United States and thus to the Great Depression.) At the same time, Frank B. Kellogg, Coolidge's secretary of state, and Aristide Briand, France's Foreign Minister, tried to persuade nations to renounce war as an instrument of policy. In 1928, 15 leading nations, among them the United States, signed the Kellogg-Briand Pact in Paris and renounced war. Almost all later participated in World War II, making the treaty seem a lie. At the time, however, it was applauded and Kellogg won the Nobel Prize for Peace.

Under Coolidge, the United States retreated from its earlier tendency to bully Latin American countries with military force. Many powerful Americans opposed the economic and social policies of the revolutionary government in Mexico, but Coolidge appointed a new ambassador, Dwight Morrow, who succeeded in solving difficulties between the two countries by negotiation, not threats. In Nicaragua, long a troubled country, Coolidge sent in the U.S. Marines to stop a civil war in 1926 but arranged for their withdrawal after free elections in 1928.

RETIREMENT. Coolidge startled political observers in the summer of 1927 by announcing that he did not "choose to run for president in 1928." He was so popular that he could easily have been reelected. In reality, he was weary of politics after his son's death and had no further goals he wished to achieve. He consented without enthusiasm to the nomination of his Secretary of Commerce Herbert Hoover as the Republican candidate. When Hoover was elected, Coolidge retired to his home in Northampton, where he wrote his autobiography and a regular newspaper column. He was in poor health and died only four years after retiring, on 5 January 1933, at his home.

When President Coolidge chose not to run for reelection, the nominee became Herbert Hoover, who was secretary of commerce in the Harding and Coolidge administrations. Coolidge accompanied Hoover in a ride from the White House to the Capitol for Hoover to be sworn in as president, 4 March 1929.

In the middle row are Senator George H. Moses of New Hampshire (left) and Representative Bertrand H. Snell of New York. They were the co-chairs of the Joint Committee on the Inaugural. (Courtesy National Archives.)

VICE PRESIDENT

Charles Gates Dawes
(1865–1951)

CHRONOLOGICAL EVENTS

1865	Born, Marietta, Ohio, 27 August
1884	Graduated from Marietta College, Ohio
1886	Graduated from Cincinnati Law School
1898	Appointed U.S. comptroller of the currency
1917	Enlisted in the U.S. Army
1921	Appointed director of the Bureau of the Budget
1924	Elected vice president
1925	Awarded the Nobel Peace Prize
1929	Appointed U.S. ambassador to Great Britain
1951	Died, Evanston, Illinois, 23 April

BIOGRAPHY

A descendant of William Dawes, who rode with Paul Revere, Charles Dawes grew up in Ohio, where his father was a lumber merchant. Dawes graduated from Marietta College and from the Cincinnati Law School. He also worked as a civil engineer for a railroad.

Settling in Lincoln, Nebraska, Dawes handled railroad rate cases. The hot-tempered Dawes frequently debated politics with another young frontier lawyer, William Jennings Bryan. Their disagreements over free silver led Dawes to research and write a book on the history of money and banking in the United States. In 1895, his business took him to Chicago, where he became treasurer for William McKinley's campaign for president—against Bryan.

President McKinley appointed Dawes comptroller of the currency. Dawes left that post to run a losing race for senator. He then organized a Chicago bank, the Central Trust Company of Illinois. During World War I, Dawes served with distinction as chief of supply procurement for the U.S. armed forces in Europe.

In 1921, President Warren G. Harding appointed Dawes to be the first director of the Bureau of the Budget. Harding later sent him to Europe as head of a commission to salvage Germany's economy. The "Dawes Plan" earned Dawes the Nobel Peace Prize in 1925.

Captivated by the active, outspoken Dawes, Republicans chose him to run with the passive, concise President Calvin Coolidge in 1924. The ticket won a landslide victory. In his inaugural speech as vice president, Dawes unexpectedly called on the U.S. Senate to abolish the filibuster and to accelerate its proceedings. Annoyed senators dismissed his advice. Neither did President Coolidge appreciate having his own address upstaged. Dawes further irritated Coolidge by declining to follow his precedent of attending cabinet meetings. Coolidge also blamed the vice president for missing a tie-breaking vote that would have confirmed the President's choice for attorney general. The two became further estranged when Dawes supported farm relief legislation that Coolidge vetoed.

Coolidge chose not to run for reelection and the Republican Party nominated Commerce Secretary Herbert Hoover for president in 1928. President Hoover appointed Dawes U.S. ambassador to Great Britain. After the Depression returned the Democrats to power, Dawes returned to his banking business in Chicago.

The Cabinet

Vice President
Charles G. Dawes, 1925

Secretary of State
Charles Evans Hughes, 1923, 1925
Frank B. Kellogg, 1925

Secretary of War
John W. Weeks, 1923, 1925
Dwight F. Davis, 1925

Secretary of the Treasury
Andrew W. Mellon, 1923, 1925

Postmaster General
Harry S. New, 1923, 1925

Attorney General
Harry M. Daugherty, 1923
Harlan Fiske Stone, 1924
John G. Sargent, 1925

Secretary of the Navy
Edwin Denby, 1923
Curtis D. Wilbur, 1924, 1925

Secretary of the Interior
Hubert Work, 1923, 1925
Roy O. West, 1928

Secretary of Agriculture
Henry C. Wallace, 1923
Howard M. Gore, 1924, 1925
William M. Jardine, 1925

Secretary of Commerce
Herbert C. Hoover, 1923, 1925
William F. Whiting, 1928

Secretary of Labor
James J. Davis, 1923, 1925

(Courtesy Herbert Hoover Presidential Library-Museum.)

Andrew W. Mellon (1855–1937). Mellon served as secretary of the treasury under Presidents Warren G. Harding, Calvin Coolidge, and Herbert Hoover (1921–1932).

Mellon's appointment by Harding astonished many for several reasons: first, most Americans had never heard of him; second, he had spent a lifetime in banking; third, he was 65 years old; and last, he was one of the richest men in the world.

As treasury secretary, Mellon's basic policies supported debt and tax reduction with special privileges for large corporations. Mellon believed that the Great Depression was part of an inevitable aftermath of World War I.

Over the years, Mellon had acquired one of the greatest private art collections. In 1937, he donated it to the National Gallery of Art in Washington, D.C.

FAMILY

CHRONOLOGICAL EVENTS

3 January 1879	Grace Anna Goodhue born
4 October 1905	Grace Goodhue married Calvin Coolidge
7 September 1906	Son, John, born
13 April 1908	Son, Calvin, Jr., born
7 July 1924	Son, Calvin, Jr., died
5 January 1933	Calvin Coolidge died
8 July 1957	Grace Coolidge died

Grace Coolidge graduated from the University of Vermont and taught at the Clarke School for the Deaf in Northampton, Massachusetts. After the President's death, she returned to Northampton and became a trustee of that school.

This is one of two paintings of Grace Coolidge by Howard Chandler Christy. Christy's first success was in illustrating Theodore Roosevelt's "Rough Riders" in Cuba during the Spanish-American War. He is best known for the painting "Signing the Constitution" which hangs in the U.S. Capitol.

Christy wanted Mrs. Coolidge to wear a red dress to contrast with her white collie, Rob Roy. President Coolidge wanted her to wear a white satin dress that he particularly liked.

"If she wears the red dress we'll have the blue sky and the white dog to make red, white, and blue," Christy argued.

"She could still wear the white dress and we'd dye the dog," the President replied. (Courtesy Library of Congress.)

The Coolidges had two sons, Calvin, Jr. (right) and John. Calvin got a blister while playing tennis at the White House. An infection set in, and he died of blood poisoning at Walter Reed Hospital at the age of 16.

John graduated from Amherst College and worked for a railroad and a printing company before retiring to Connecticut. His wife, Florence Trumbull, was the daughter of the governor of Connecticut. (Courtesy Library of Congress.)

PLACES

THE CALVIN COOLIDGE BIRTHPLACE AND HOMESTEAD

The Plymouth Notch Historic District • P.O. Box 79 • Plymouth, Vermont 05056 • Tel: (802) 672-3773

Located 6 miles south of U.S. Route 4, on Vermont Route 100A, approximately 14 miles southeast of Rutland. Open daily, 27 May through 15 October, from 9:30 A.M. to 5:30 P.M. Admission fee, with discounts available for children and registered groups of 15 or more. Family passes available. The visitor center contains a museum, a gift shop, and a lounge. For more information, write: Vermont Division for Historic Preservation, 135 State Street, Drawer 33, Montpelier, VT 05633-1201. Owned and operated by the State of Vermont, Division for Historic Preservation.

◀ *In 1968, the State of Vermont acquired the birthplace and began an extensive renovation. Old photographs were used as a guide to restore it to its 1872 appearance. It is now furnished with original artifacts donated by the Coolidge family.* (Courtesy Vermont Division for Historic Preservation, President Calvin Coolidge State Historic Site.)

▲ *Vice President Coolidge took the oath of office here as President of the United States at 2:47 A.M. on 3 August 1923.* (Courtesy Vermont Division for Historic Preservation, President Calvin Coolidge State Historic Site; photographer: William Jenney.)

The birthplace is a five-room house attached to the general store that Coolidge's father, John, operated. Calvin Coolidge was born in the downstairs bedroom on 4 July 1872. Four years later, his family moved across the street to what is now known as the Coolidge Homestead. In 1968, the Vermont Division for Historic Preservation purchased the birthplace and general store and restored the building to its 1872 appearance. The furnishings were donated by the Coolidge family.

The homestead was purchased by Coolidge's father in 1876. It was Coolidge's boyhood home. In 1923, while he was vacationing there, he was administered the presidential oath of office by his father. His father lived in the house until his death in 1926. In 1931, Coolidge built an addition which was removed when the house was given to the State of Vermont in 1956 by his son, John, and his daughter-in-law, Florence. It has been restored to its appearance in 1923. All the original furnishings are preserved.

Herbert Hoover

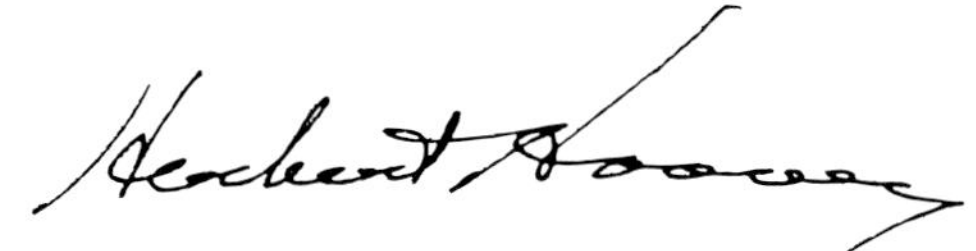

CHRONOLOGICAL EVENTS

11 August 1874	Born, West Branch, Iowa
29 May 1895	Graduated from Stanford University, Palo Alto, California
1896	Mining engineer, Australia
June 1900	Witnessed the Boxer Rebellion, China
1903–1917	Lived in London, England
1914	Organized American Relief Committee, London, England
October 1914	Named director of the Commission for Relief in Belgium
19 May 1917	Appointed director of the U.S. Food Administration
5 March 1921	Appointed secretary of commerce
1922	Published *American Individualism*
1927	Directed Mississippi Flood Relief programs
6 November 1928	Elected president
4 March 1929	Inaugurated president
15 June 1929	Signed Agricultural Marketing Act
29 October 1929	Stock Market Crash
June 1930	Signed Smoot-Hawley Tariff
22 July 1930	Signed London Naval Treaty
26 February 1931	Vetoed veterans' bonus bill
22 January 1932	Signed Reconstruction Finance Corporation Act
28 July 1932	Dispatched federal troops to disperse Bonus Army
8 November 1932	Defeated for reelection as president
1933	Retired to Palo Alto, California
1934	Published *The Challenge to Liberty*
1947	Appointed chairman of the Commission on Organization of the Executive Branch of the Government (the Hoover Commission)
1951	Published *The Memoirs of Herbert Hoover*
1958	Published *The Ordeal of Wilson*
20 October 1964	Died, New York, New York

BIOGRAPHY

Herbert Hoover was a man of remarkable achievements. He mobilized private and public aid to war-torn countries. He developed ways for government to help businesses obtain accurate data and manufacture safe products. He helped redesign the United States Government. But his presidency was one of the most disappointing in U.S. history. This gifted man proved unable to deal with the Great Depression, the huge economic crisis that overtook the United States and the world during his administration. As a result, he left office scorned by many Americans. He recovered their respect only later in his long life.

CHILDHOOD. Herbert Clark Hoover was born 11 August 1874 in the Quaker community of West Branch, Iowa. He was the second son of Jesse Hoover, a blacksmith, and Hulda Minthorn. Both parents came from Quaker families whose members were deeply involved in charities and missionary work. Both parents died before he was 10 years old, and young Hoover was sent to Oregon to live with his uncle, John Minthorn, a physician and real estate promoter. He lived first in Newberg and then in Salem, the state capital.

COLLEGE. At age 16 and without having completed high school, Hoover was admitted to the new, tuition-free Leland Stanford University in Palo Alto, California, which was seeking students from the West. He majored in geology. Hardworking and thrifty, Hoover paid for his own college expenses by taking on-campus jobs during the school year and by doing summer work with the U.S. Geological Survey. At Stanford he met his future wife, Lou Henry, the daughter of an Iowa banker. She was also a geology major.

MINING ENGINEER. Hoover graduated from Stanford in 1895, in the middle of a national economic slump. He worked as a miner in the gold mines of northern California for several months and then became an assistant to Louis Janin, a San Francisco mining consultant. In October 1896, Janin recommended him for an engineering position with a British gold mining company in Coolgardie, Australia. Hoover spent two years there. He was very successful and although he was only in his early twenties, he was named the company's representative in China. Before he went to China, he went to California and married Lou Henry.

The Hoovers remained in China for four years. While there, they were threatened by the anti-Western Boxer Rebellion. Hoover rose to become a partner in the company and founded a company to help the Chinese Government develop its coal mines. In 1903, the Hoovers moved to London, which became their home for the next 14 years. Hoover kept his U.S. citizenship and owned a house in California to which he intended to return when his business made it possible. But from 1903 to 1914, he traveled widely as a mining consultant. He became a millionaire, making money especially from mining operations in Burma and Russia. He and Mrs. Hoover were accepted into upper-class British society, despite Hoover's curt, abrupt manner, which offended some people. The two completed and published in 1912 a translation of *De Re Metallica*, a sixteenth-century Latin classic on mining.

WORLD WAR I. In the summer of 1914 war began in Europe. London was soon full of stranded U.S. tourists in need of help to get home. Hoover volunteered to collect funds and organize help for them. His success in this effort led to his being approached by a group of U.S. and Belgian citizens called the Commission for Relief in Belgium (CBR). Belgium had been overrun early in the war by the German army and many of its people were starving. Since the United States was neutral in the war, Germany was willing to allow Americans to collect food to be used to relieve hunger in Belgium. The task appealed to Hoover's Quaker belief in serving humanity and helping needy people. He accepted it willingly and headed the CBR until 1917, when the United States entered the war. His work saved hundreds of thousands of lives. His manner, however, was unusual for the director of a large charitable enterprise. He was matter-of-fact and businesslike, not sympathetic or compassionate.

When the United States declared war on Germany in April 1917, President Woodrow Wilson asked Hoover to come home and take a leading position in the war government. Hoover became director of the U.S. Food Administration, a new post with broad powers, created to meet wartime needs. His appointment was popular with the public, who regarded him as a hero for his work in Belgium. As food administrator, Hoover stressed voluntary public cooperation. His advertising urged Americans to eat less and to moderate their consumption to wartime needs. He set food prices by negotiation with businesses rather than by legal action. His workload was heavy and complicated, and he handled it well.

At the end of the war in 1918, Wilson named Hoover to administer U.S. food relief to the starving European nations. The task was enormous. Much of eastern and southern Europe was still at war, although the major powers had ceased fighting. The performance of Hoover and his group, the American Relief Administration, was remarkable. They delivered $5 billion in U.S. aid, restored communications, reopened coal mines, and supplied medical needs.

ELECTION OF 1920. President Wilson became ill as his second term drew to an end and there was much discussion about possible successors. Hoover had come to be a public figure of such stature that many Americans mentioned him as a possible candidate, although no one knew to which political party he belonged. He finally announced early in 1920 that he was a Republican but that he strongly favored Wilson's plan for a League of Nations, which most Republicans opposed. His stand was popular with the public but not with Republican politicians. The Republican nomination went to Senator Warren G. Harding of Ohio, who won the presidential election.

SECRETARY OF COMMERCE. Harding immediately asked Hoover to be part of his cabinet and offered him his choice of departments: Interior or Commerce. Hoover chose Commerce. This seemed a minor position, but Hoover had big plans for it.

Herbert Hoover (right) was appointed secretary of commerce by President Warren G. Harding in 1921. After Harding's death, Hoover retained his post in the administration of Calvin Coolidge (left). In 1927, Hoover became the leading candidate for the Republican presidential nomination after Coolidge announced that he would not seek renomination. (Courtesy Library of Congress.)

He hoped to use it to revitalize the relationship between the government and U.S. business. He also hoped to become a leading adviser to the President.

Hoover was successful in both aims. He stayed at the Commerce Department for more than six years and became a leading adviser to Harding and then to Harding's successor, Calvin Coolidge. He transformed the Census Bureau into a major supplier of statistical information for U.S. businesses. The Bureau of Standards, under his leadership, worked with the business community to develop a long list of product design and safety standards. Under Hoover's guidance the government began regulating the broadcasting industry with the Radio Act of 1927, drawn up by Hoover's department.

Hoover's activities regularly extended beyond the Commerce Department into other fields. He was active in labor-management relations; he persuaded the steel industry to abolish the 12-hour day. He vigorously promoted bills for a dam on the Colorado River, a St. Lawrence Seaway to link Great Lakes shipping with the Atlantic Ocean, and pollution control. He took a vigorous role in relieving floods on the Mississippi River in 1927. He was, in short, one of the leading Republican policymakers of the 1920s.

ELECTION OF 1928. President Coolidge unexpectedly announced in 1927 that he did not plan

The Philosophy of Rugged Individualism

. . . It is a false liberalism that interprets itself into the government operation of commercial business. Every step of bureaucratizing of the business of our country poisons the very roots of liberalism—that is, political equality, free speech, free assembly, free press, and equality of opportunity. It is the road not to more liberty, but to less liberty. Liberalism should be found not striving to spread bureaucracy but striving to set bounds to it. True liberalism seeks all legitimate freedom first in the confident belief that without such freedom the pursuit of all other blessings and benefits is vain. That belief is the foundation of all American progress, political as well as economic.

Liberalism is a force truly of the spirit, a force proceeding from the deep realization that economic freedom cannot be sacrificed if political freedom is to be preserved. Even if Governmental conduct of business could give us more efficiency instead of less efficiency, the fundamental objection to it would remain unaltered and unabated. It would destroy political equality. It would increase rather than decrease abuse and corruption. It would stifle initiative and invention. It would undermine the development of leadership. It would cramp and cripple the mental and spiritual energies of our people. It would extinguish equality and opportunity. It would dry up the spirit of liberty and progress. For these reasons primarily it must be resisted. For a hundred and fifty years liberalism has found its true spirit in the American system, not in the European systems. . . .

Nor do I wish to be misinterpreted as believing that the United States is free-for-all and devil-take-the-hindmost. The very essence of equality of opportunity and of American individualism is that there shall be no domination by any group or combination in this republic, whether it be business or political. On the contrary, it demands economic justice as well as political and social justice. It is no system of laissez faire (government non interference in the affairs of big business). . . .

• *Herbert Hoover delivered this speech in New York City on 22 October 1928. He condemned the Democratic platform as state socialism and upheld free competition and private initiative as the traditional American way.*

ACCEPTANCE SPEECH

. . . Across the path of the nation's consideration of these vast problems of economic and social order, there has arisen a bitter controversy over the control of the liquor traffic. I have always sympathized with the high purpose of the Eighteenth Amendment, and I have used every power at my command to make it effective, over the entire country. I have hoped it was the final solution of the evils of the liquor traffic against which our people have striven for generations. It has succeeded in great measure in those many communities where the majority sentiment is favorable to it. But in other and increasing number of communities there is a majority sentiment unfavorable to it. Laws opposed by majority sentiment create resentment which undermines enforcement and in the end produces degeneration and crime.

We must recognize the difficulties which have developed in making the Eighteenth Amendment effective, and that grave abuses have grown up. In order to secure the enforcement of the Amendment under our dual form of government the constitutional provision called for concurrent action on the one hand by the state and local authorities and on the other by the Federal government. Its enforcement requires independent but coincident action of both agencies. An increasing number of states and municipalities are proving themselves unwilling to engage in such enforcement. Due to these forces there is in large sections an increasing illegal traffic in liquor. But worse than this there has been in those areas a spread of disrespect not only for this law but for all laws, grave dangers of practical nullification of the Constitution, a degeneration in municipal government, and an increase in subsidized crime and violence. I can not consent to the continuation of this regime. . . .

I refuse . . . on the one hand to return to the old saloon with its political and social corruption, or on the other to endure the bootlegger and the speakeasy with their abuses and crime. Either is intolerable. These are not the ways out.

The Republican platform recommends submission of the question to the states, that the people themselves may determine whether they desire a change. . . .

• *Hoover delivered his acceptance speech to the Republican convention on 11 August 1928. Prohibition was an issue in the 1928 election. Both Hoover and Alfred E. Smith promised to enforce the Eighteenth Amendment (prohibition). Smith, however, thought Congress could allow states to sell wines and beers if they chose to.*

to seek renomination. Hoover, as the best known member of his popular administration, was Coolidge's logical successor. Hoover had drawbacks as a candidate: he was personally shy, had few political skills, and had never been elected to public office. But these were outweighed by public respect for his abilities. The Republican convention nominated him for president and named Senator Charles Curtis of Nebraska as his running mate. The Democratic candidate, Governor Alfred E. Smith of New York, held positions similar to Hoover's on most major issues. On Prohibition, however, Smith was a "wet"—he believed that the national effort to end the use of alcoholic beverages by law had failed and should be repealed. As an urban Catholic, he was a menacing figure to some rural voters. Hoover continued to approve of Prohibition as "an experiment noble in purpose." This stand won Democratic votes for him in the South. With the general prosperity in the country,

Hoover was a popular candidate. He defeated Smith easily, 444 electoral votes to 87.

PRESIDENT. Hoover entered office with clear plans for reforming the government and the economy. He wanted a separate department of health and education and increased funding for the Children's Bureau, the first federal social welfare agency. He wanted a system of farmers' cooperatives with power to stabilize commodity prices. He had plans to expand the National Park Service and to give more personal freedom and individual ownership to Native Americans on federal reservations. With regard to Prohibition, Hoover hoped to study government efforts and decide whether the policy was really enforceable or whether it should be discontinued. He accomplished many of these reforms; only the department of health and education failed to become a reality. Most of his presidency, however, was dominated by the problems of the Great Depression.

THE GREAT DEPRESSION. The Great Depression began dramatically in October 1929 with a rapid drop in stock prices on the New York Stock Exchange. Such an event had always heralded some sort of slowdown in U.S. business, and for the next 18 months industries across the United States cut back production and laid off workers, while government tax revenues declined. Hoover, like most businessmen, saw these developments as a natural part of the economic cycle. He insisted that the public did not need to be alarmed, describing the process as a "depression" rather than as a "panic," the word used previously in U.S. politics. In public statements he emphasized his belief, shared with most informed Americans, that the business readjustment would end soon. (He did not, however, say, "Prosperity is just around the corner"; that was a phrase of Vice President Curtis.)

In May 1931, the Kreditanstalt bank in Vienna failed, setting off a financial crisis in Europe. Panicked Europeans withdrew their money from U.S. banks and stopped buying U.S. goods. Their actions redoubled the problems facing U.S. bankers, manufacturers, and laborers. Unemployment increased dramatically, cities and states began going bankrupt, and U.S. industrial production shrank to a small fraction of capacity. For the last two years of Hoover's presidency, the U.S. economy was clearly in a major crisis, and "depression" became a synonym for disaster.

Even in the early stages of the Depression, Hoover acted vigorously. Immediately after the stock market crash, he arranged for a pool of businessmen to raise $300 million to keep stock prices from falling further. The intervention

EXCERPT FROM *THE MEMOIRS OF HERBERT HOOVER*

"In the large sense the primary cause of the Great Depression was the war of 1914–1918. Without the war there would have been no depression of such dimensions. There might have been a normal cyclical recession; but, with the usual timing, even that readjustment probably would not have taken place at that particular period, nor would it have been a 'Great Depression.'

The Great Depression was a two-stage process of several phases. We had a normal recession due to domestic causes beginning with the stock-market slump in October, 1929, but we were on the way out of it when the European difficulties rose to hurricane force and struck us in April, 1931. Thus the Great Depression did not really begin in the United States until the European collapse."

• *The Great Depression was world wide. Historians and economists continue to disagree as to what caused it. Hoover, however, placed the primary cause on the devastation created by World War I. What is remarkable is not that the Depression occurred but that it was so severe and that it lasted so long.*

(Courtesy National Archives.)

In 1928, Congress authorized the Boulder Dam project in Black Canyon on the Colorado River. Construction began in 1931 and was completed in 1936. The entire cost of the project cost approximately $385 million.

Ray Lyman Wilbur, Hoover's secretary of the interior, renamed the project the Hoover Dam in 1930. In a mean-spirited political act, Franklin D. Roosevelt's Secretary of the Interior Harold Ickes ordered on 8 May 1933 that the dam be known as Boulder Dam rather than Hoover Dam. He said that Hoover had nothing to do with conceiving it or getting the authorization of Congress for its construction. Ickes also claimed that it was not right for one of Hoover's cabinet members to name a dam after the President.

Ickes was wrong on all counts. In his Memoirs, *Hoover pointed out "the custom of naming great water conservation dams after the Presidents in whose administrations they were undertaken. That had been the case with Theodore Roosevelt, Taft, Wilson, and Coolidge." He went on to say that the name was changed under orders from President Roosevelt, who was trying to smear his reputation. Roosevelt dedicated the dam without even mentioning Hoover. The name was restored by unanimous action of the House of Representatives in 1947. Congressman Jack Z. Anderson had introduced the bill and notified Hoover.*

The former President replied:

March 10, 1947

My Dear Mr. Congressman:

Thank you for yours of March seventh.

Confidentially, having had streets, parks, school houses, hills, and valleys named for me, as is done to all Presidents, I have not thought this item of great importance in the life of a nation. But when a President of the United States tears one's name down, that is a public defamation and an insult. Therefore, I am grateful to you for removing it.

Yours faithfully,
Herbert Hoover

worked, and the fall in prices stopped temporarily. He called manufacturers to the White House and had them pledge not to cut wages during the economic slowdown. They kept this promise until 1932. Although many industrial workers were laid off, those who kept their jobs earned excellent wages.

At the same time, Hoover speeded up action on a number of government construction projects, such as the Golden Gate Bridge, linking San Francisco and Oakland, Boulder Dam on the Colorado River, and the redevelopment of downtown Washington, D.C., to increase the number of jobs and to put government money into the economy. His new Agricultural Marketing Act, passed before the Depression began, used government loans through farmers' cooperatives to keep up the prices of farm products. These policies were strongly criticized as wasteful by many Democrats, who felt that a balanced budget was the most important national goal.

Hoover received little credit for these efforts, largely because of his lack of political skill. He was a blunt, curt, and very private man who found it difficult to project an image of warmth and sympathy. Many reporters disliked him and portrayed him unfairly. His background in business was also a disadvantage, as the public held corrupt, greedy businessmen responsible for the Depression. As the Depression continued, several writers published books about him that falsely depicted him as crooked and unethical. After 1931 much of the public had turned against him.

One government action in response to the Depression was poorly conceived and damaging. In 1930, Congress passed the Smoot-Hawley Tariff. Anxious to protect U.S. farmers and manufacturers, Congress raised tariffs to the highest level in U.S. history. Hoover disapproved of the bill, but he signed it anyway, because it gave him some power to adjust tariff rates. The tariff offended other countries that traded with the United States and were having their own economic difficulties. By slowing down world trade, the bill contributed to the European collapse of 1931.

As the Depression deepened in 1931, Hoover asked for and received more power from

PRESS STATEMENT

This is not an issue as to whether people shall go hungry or cold in the United States. It is solely a question of the best method by which hunger and cold shall be prevented. It is a question as to whether the American people on one hand will maintain the spirit of charity and mutual self help through voluntary giving and the responsibility of local government as distinguished on the other hand from appropriations out of the Federal Treasury for such purposes. My own conviction is strongly that if we break down this sense of responsibility of individual generosity to individual and mutual self help in the country in times of national difficulty and if we start appropriations of this character we have not only impaired something infinitely valuable in the life of the American people but have struck at the roots of self-government. Once this has happened it is not the cost of a few score millions but we are faced with the abyss of reliance in future upon Government charity in some form or other. The money involved is indeed the least of the costs to American ideals and American institutions.

• *Hoover issued this statement on 3 February 1931. He opposed direct federal aid for unemployed Americans on the grounds that it would weaken their self-respect. He thought that it would undermine private charities and would destroy the American tradition of local care for the needy.*

EXCERPT FROM *THE MEMOIRS OF HERBERT HOOVER*

"Probably the greatest coup of all was the distortion of the story of the Bonus March on Washington in July, 1932. About 11,000 supposed veterans congregated in Washington to urge action by Congress to pay a deferred war bonus in cash instead of over a period of years.

The Democratic leaders did not organize the Bonus March nor conduct the ensuing riots. But the Democratic organization seized upon the incident with great avidity. Many Democratic speakers in the campaign of 1932 implied that I had murdered veterans on the streets of Washington.

The story was kept alive for twenty years. I, therefore, deal with it at greater length than would otherwise be warranted. As abundantly proved later on, the march was in considerable part organized and promoted by the Communists and included a large number of hoodlums and ex-convicts determined to raise a public disturbance. They were frequently addressed by Democratic Congressmen seeking to inflame them against me for my opposition to the bonus legislation. They were given financial support by some of the publishers of the sensational press. It was of interest to learn in after years from the Communist confessions that they also had put on a special battery of speakers to help Roosevelt in his campaign, by the use of the incident.

When it was evident that no legislation on the bonus would be passed by Congress, I asked the chairmen of the Congressional committees to appropriate funds to buy tickets home for the legitimate veterans. This was done and some 6,000 availed themselves of its aid, leaving about 5,000 mixed hoodlums, ex-convicts, Communists, and a minority of veterans in Washington. Through government agencies we obtained the names of upwards of 2,000 of those remaining and found that fewer than a third of them had ever served in the armies, and that over 900 on the basis of this sampling were ex-convicts and Communists."

▲ *The Bonus Marchers were dispersed by General Douglas MacArthur (right) and Major Dwight D. Eisenhower (left, standing behind unidentified man) on 29 July 1932. President Hoover's harshness in handling these veterans and their families created the image of an insensitive president.* (Courtesy National Archives.)

• *Hoover maintained that the Bonus Army was part of a communist conspiracy to overthrow the U.S. Government. He never changed his mind on this point despite charges of insensitivity.*

Congress to combat it. His main agency was the Reconstruction Finance Corporation (RFC), which could make massive loans to banks and state governments to get more money into the economy. The RFC had vast powers but used them too slowly and sparingly to be effective.

Hoover was bitterly criticized then and later for ignoring the human suffering, unemployment, and hunger caused by the Depression and for treating it simply as a problem in business credit. He resisted suggestions for direct federal aid to needy individuals. To many he seemed cold-hearted. The reasons for his attitude were complex. He feared that if government, by direct aid to the needy, became dominant in the economy, special interests like business or labor might attempt to take over its power and eventually impose a fascist government. But he never succeeded in expressing this view convincingly to the public.

The Bonus March of July 1932 further damaged Hoover's public image. Thousands of World War I veterans and their families came to Washington to demand that Congress pass a bill to speed up the distribution of bonuses for their military service which were scheduled to be awarded in 1945. They camped in a makeshift tent city south of the

President Hoover signed the Naval Disarmament Treaty on 22 July 1930 in the East Room of the White House. Japan later renounced the treaty and a naval arms race began.

Standing, left to right, Senator Joseph T. Robinson; Secretary of State Henry L. Stimson; Vice President Charles Curtis; Senator William E. Borah, chairman of the Committee on Foreign Relations; Senator Claude A. Swanson; Secretary of the Navy Charles F. Adams; Senator James E. Watson; and Senator David A. Reed.

(Courtesy Herbert Hoover Presidential Library-Museum.)

Capitol. Hoover had been generous with veterans —veterans' benefits accounted for one fourth of the federal budget—but he opposed this bill. So did Congress, which rejected it. When some of the marchers began surrounding the Capitol and intimidating legislators, Hoover ordered army units under General Douglas MacArthur to disperse them. In the ensuing conflict, one demonstrator was killed and the tent city was burned. The action, which seemed cruel and heavy-handed, probably destroyed Hoover's chances of reelection. When his Democratic opponent, Franklin Roosevelt, heard what had happened, he turned to a companion and said, "This will elect me."

FOREIGN POLICY. Hoover's foreign policy focused on peace. He tried to avoid military action and to eliminate the causes of war. He began withdrawing U.S. troops from Haiti and assured Latin American leaders that he would not interfere in their affairs as previous U.S. presidents in the twentieth century had done. He arranged disarmament talks with Great Britain and Japan, concluding the London Naval Treaty, which was effective for only a short time. In the Far East, he did not respond with force to Japan's attacks on China but simply expressed U.S. disapproval.

Most of his international activity, however, dealt with the effects of the Depression abroad. When financial crisis hit Europe in 1931, Hoover announced a one-year suspension on payments of all World War I debts and reparations. This bold measure by the leading creditor nation probably saved Europe from falling into financial chaos. Hoover's other major effort, to keep all the major powers' economies tied to the gold standard, was less successful. In September 1931, the British Government, hoping to save Great Britain's economic position, abandoned the gold standard and let its currency depreciate. This action caused great instability in world financial markets, which lasted through the rest of Hoover's term.

ELECTION OF 1932. The Republican Party

Excerpt from *The Memoirs of Herbert Hoover*

"One of Roosevelt's most effective campaign issues was of course the depression. His strategy was to allege that I had made the depression and then done nothing about it. He stated six varieties of 'proofs' and 'causes' for which I was responsible: First, that the depression was entirely of domestic origin; Second, that I was personally responsible for the stock market boom and the orgy of speculation; Third, that as Secretary of Commerce I had caused the overbuilding of industry; Fourth, that as Secretary of Commerce I had been responsible for private loans to foreigners which by their default were a cause of the depression; Fifth, that the Smoot-Hawley Tariff had destroyed our foreign markets, drained the world of gold, made it impossible for foreigners to pay their debts, and started trade reprisals over the world; and Sixth, that by extravagance and reckless spending I had created a great Federal deficit which was strangling the country.

The miseries of the people and the wrongdoing of business (mostly exposed by my administration), with the help of innuendo and sly inference, furnished magnificent oratorical material for emotionalizing these issues."

- *During the 1932 campaign, Hoover attacked the Democrats as dangerous radicals. He tried to explain away the Depression and he asked that people not hold him responsible. In his* Memoirs, *he criticizes Franklin D. Roosevelt's betrayal of him and "for emotionalizing these issues."*

renominated Hoover in 1932 without enthusiasm. No other leading Republican wanted the nomination. Republicans knew that, as the party of business, they had become unpopular and were likely to lose the election. The Democrats chose Governor Franklin D. Roosevelt of New York to run against Hoover. To a large degree, the campaign centered on Hoover's personal unpopularity. Roosevelt did not need to offer a coherent plan to combat the Depression to be a credible candidate, and he offered no such plan. In November, he defeated Hoover, 472 electoral votes to 59.

AFTER THE ELECTION. Hoover's defeat came as the Depression moved into a new phase. Across the nation, banks were running short of funds. Many were forced to close, and depositors lost their money. Under the Constitution, Hoover's term lasted until 4 March 1933. Although a defeated president, he had the responsibility for dealing with the bank crisis for four more months. He tried to work out with Roosevelt a joint plan of action for that time. He hoped to persuade Roosevelt, whom he considered irresponsible and inexperienced, to accept parts of his own plan. Roosevelt carefully avoided committing himself. As a result, little was done. The crisis intensified until 4 March, when Roosevelt was inaugurated and a bitter Hoover left Washington. As a result of Hoover's experience, the Constitution was amended to make the transition period shorter. The outgoing president's term now ends on 20 January.

POST PRESIDENTIAL YEARS. Hoover retired to California, where he busied himself setting up the Hoover Institution on War, Revolution, and Peace, at Stanford. He was bitterly critical of Roosevelt's anti-Depression program, the New Deal, and frequently spoke against it. The ill feeling was mutual. When World War II broke out, Hoover, despite his experience, was not asked to serve in any public position.

Roosevelt's successor, Harry Truman, made more use of Hoover's talents. After World War II ended, Truman asked Hoover to take charge of food relief in war-torn Europe. Hoover did so as effectively as ever. In 1947, Truman appointed him chairman of a bipartisan commission to reduce waste, prevent duplication, and increase efficiency in the rapidly expanding federal government. The Hoover Commission's recommendations, most of which were adopted, saved the government several billion dollars.

After his wife's death in 1944, Hoover moved to New York, where he spent the last years of his life. In the 1950s, he served on another, less successful, Hoover Commission for President Dwight D. Eisenhower. He also wrote several books on his World War I experiences and on the presidency of Woodrow Wilson. He died 20 October 1964 in New York. He had lived longer after his presidency than any other person who had held the office.

VICE PRESIDENT

Charles Curtis
(1860–1936)

CHRONOLOGICAL EVENTS

1860	Born, Topeka, Kansas, 25 January
1884	Elected prosecuting attorney of Shawnee County, Kansas
1892	Elected to U.S. House of Representatives
1907	Elected to U.S. Senate
1925	Elected Senate majority leader
1928	Elected vice president
1936	Died, Washington, D.C., 8 February

BIOGRAPHY

The son of a white man and a Native American woman, Charles Curtis spent much of his childhood on the Kaw reservation. Learning to ride horses at the reservation, Curtis became a successful jockey who was known around Kansas as "the Indian Boy."

His Native American grandmother persuaded him to leave the reservation and get a formal education. Living with his white grandparents in Topeka, he went to high school and then worked as a custodian at a law firm while he studied law. In 1884, Curtis won election as county attorney. A conservative Republican, he opposed the Populist movement that was sweeping across Kansas. In 1892, he defeated a fusion Democrat and Populist candidate to win election to the U.S. House of Representatives.

As a member of the House Committee on Indian Affairs, he wrote the Curtis Act in 1898, which increased federal authority over Indian lands. Elected to the U.S. Senate, Curtis helped enact the Payne-Aldrich Tariff of 1909, whose high rates increased the split between the Republicans' progressive and conservative wings. That split cost him renomination in 1912. In 1914, he won one of the first popular elections for the Senate.

Senate Republicans elected Curtis their whip and later their majority leader. Both progressive and conservative senators found him true to his word and "unusually adept at making deals." As a Kansan, Curtis supported farm relief, but when President Calvin Coolidge vetoed the McNary-Haugen bill, the majority leader cast the vote that narrowly sustained Coolidge's veto.

In 1928, Curtis tried for the Republican presidential nomination. He directed much criticism at the front-runner, Herbert Hoover. When Hoover took the nomination, Republicans chose Curtis for vice president, but the two men never forgot that they had campaigned against each other. Despite Curtis's long experience in Congress, Hoover rarely asked his advice on legislation.

The widower vice president became involved in an embarrassing quarrel over protocol when his sister, Dolly Gans, demanded a higher social rank than the wife of the House Speaker. Such public feuding made Curtis look foolish in the press. His image slipped further when World War I Bonus Marchers surrounded the Capitol in 1932 to demand help from Congress and a panicking Curtis called out the Marines to protect the Capitol.

Defeated for reelection, Curtis opened a law practice in Washington. In 1935, he became chairman of the Republican Senatorial Campaign Committee, but he died before the 1936 election.

THE CABINET

SECRETARY OF STATE
Henry L. Stimson, 1929

SECRETARY OF WAR
James W. Good, 1929
Patrick J. Hurley, 1929

SECRETARY OF THE TREASURY
Andrew W. Mellon, 1929
Ogden L. Mills, 1932

POSTMASTER GENERAL
Walter F. Brown, 1929

ATTORNEY GENERAL
William DeWitt Mitchell, 1929

SECRETARY OF THE NAVY
Charles Francis Adams, 1929

SECRETARY OF THE INTERIOR
Ray L. Wilbur, 1929

SECRETARY OF AGRICULTURE
Arthur M. Hyde, 1929

SECRETARY OF COMMERCE
Robert P. Lamont, 1929
Roy D. Chapin, 1932

SECRETARY OF LABOR
James J. Davis, 1929
William N. Doak, 1930

Charles Francis Adams (1866–1954). Adams was appointed secretary of the navy by President Herbert Hoover in 1929.

Adams was the great-great-grandson of President John Adams, and the great-grandson of President John Quincy Adams. He was the third prominent Adams to bear the name Charles Francis, after his grandfather, the diplomat (1807–1886) and his lawyer-historian uncle (1835–1915).

From 1900 until the end of his life, Adams was a director of leading U.S. banks and corporations.

Under Adams's tenure as navy secretary, budget cutbacks during the Depression forced major reductions in shipbuilding. The corresponding revival of Japanese militarism became Adams's chief concern. He repeatedly pleaded with Congress for more naval appropriations.

Adams (right) is shown here with President Hoover and Secretary of War Henry L. Stimson (left). (Courtesy Herbert Hoover Presidential Library-Museum.)

FAMILY

CHRONOLOGICAL EVENTS

29 March 1874	Lou Henry born
10 February 1899	Lou Henry married Herbert Hoover
4 August 1903	Son, Herbert, Jr., born
17 July 1907	Son, Allan, born
7 January 1944	Lou Hoover died
20 October 1964	Herbert Hoover died

(Courtesy Library of Congress.)

Lou Henry met Herbert Hoover in a geology laboratory at Stanford University where they were both students. She was a freshman; he was a senior. They were married five years later, when she graduated.

They immediately left for China which was the beginning of their travels all over the world. She learned many languages including Chinese and Latin. She learned Latin to help her husband translate a sixteenth-century work on mining, geology, and metallurgy.

She helped Hoover in his European relief programs during World War I. The family moved to Washington in 1921, when President Warren G. Harding appointed Hoover secretary of commerce. After Roosevelt's Inauguration in 1933, they returned to Palo Alto, California, where they had been students.

Both sons were born in London and both graduated from Stanford University. Herbert Hoover, Jr. was an engineer and a diplomat. President Dwight D. Eisenhower appointed him undersecretary of state for Middle Eastern affairs in 1954. Allan Hoover got his M.B.A. from Harvard and became a mining engineer.

Herbert Hoover National Historic Site

P.O. Box 607
West Branch, Iowa 52358
Tel: (319) 643-2541

The Herbert Hoover birthplace cottage stands on its original site at the corner of Downey and Penn streets in West Branch, Iowa. (Courtesy National Park Service.) ▶

Located half a mile north of Interstate 80, off Exit 254, just east of Iowa City. Open daily from 9 A.M. to 5 P.M. Closed Thanksgiving, Christmas, and New Year's Day. Admission fee, with discounts available for senior citizens. Children ages 15 and under admitted free. Tours available for groups of 15 or more, with advance reservations. The 186-acre site contains Hoover's birthplace, a blacksmith shop, a one-room schoolhouse, a meetinghouse, the graves of President and Mrs. Hoover, a visitor center, and the Hoover Presidential Library–Museum. Administered by the National Park Service, U.S. Department of the Interior.

Herbert Hoover was born on 10 August 1874 in a two-room cottage on Downey Street in West Branch, Iowa. The 14-by-20-foot cottage was built by his father, Jesse, and his grandfather, Eli, in 1871. Eight years later, the family sold it and moved into a larger home farther south on Downey Street. In 1939, the birthplace cottage was restored to its 1874 appearance. Original furnishings were used as much as possible. In 1964, it was designated a National Historic Site.

Herbert Hoover died on 20 October 1964. Five days later, he was buried on a hillside approximately one quarter of a mile southwest of the birthplace cottage. The body of Mrs. Hoover, who had died in 1944, was reburied there at that time.

▲ *The Friends Meetinghouse was built in 1857 and restored by the Herbert Hoover Foundation in 1964. During Hoover's childhood years in West Branch, Iowa, he worshipped there with his family. His mother, Hulda, was a minister at this Quaker Meetinghouse. It has been moved about two blocks from its original location.* (Courtesy National Park Service.)

The Herbert Hoover Presidential Library and Museum

P.O. Box 488 • West Branch, Iowa 52358 • Tel: (319) 643-5301

Located on the Herbert Hoover National Historic Site. Open daily from 9 A.M. to 5 P.M. Closed Thanksgiving, Christmas, and New Year's Day. Admission fee for museum only. Tours available for groups of 15 or more, with advance reservations. Administered by the National Archives and Records Administration.

▲ *The suite at the Waldorf Towers in New York where the former president lived is re-created in the museum.* (Courtesy National Park Service.)

The library houses a collection of manuscripts and papers accumulated by Hoover during his 50 years of public service. It also holds approximately 20,000 books and objects associated with his career, in addition to photograph and film collections and special exhibits. A 180-seat auditorium is located on the premises. The library–museum, built by the Herbert Hoover Birthplace Foundation, was dedicated in 1962.

◀ *Herbert Hoover died on 20 October 1964. His body lay in state for two days at the Capitol Rotunda in Washington, D.C. On 25 October, he was buried within sight of the cottage where he was born. His wife, Lou, had died 20 years earlier and was buried in Palo Alto, California. Following the President's death, her body was moved and placed next to him in West Branch, Iowa.* (Courtesy National Park Service.)

THEODORE ROOSEVELT

Jean Fritz's *Bully for You, Teddy Roosevelt* (G. P. Putnam's Sons, 1991) is an entertaining story of one of the country's more colorful presidents. Nancy Whitelaw's *Theodore Roosevelt Takes Charge* (Albert Whitman, 1992) is an excellent biography that emphasizes his life before the presidency. (For junior high school.)

Theodore Roosevelt and His America by Milton Meltzer (Watts, 1994) is a vivid portrait of this charismatic leader. It puts Roosevelt's life and presidency into perspective as the country changed from an agrarian to an industrial economy. *Mornings on Horseback* by David McCullough (Simon & Schuster, 1981) chronicles the young Roosevelt's experiences growing up out West as he struggled with asthma and strove to develop of self-reliance. (For junior and senior high school.)

Roosevelt's Rough Riders by Virgil C. Jones (Doubleday, 1971) is a full account, told from the perspective of an enlisted man, of a most unusual regiment; it existed for only 137 days. *Theodore Roosevelt: The Making of a Conservationist* (University of Illinois Press, 1985) is an excellent biography that concentrates on the years before he became president. Edmund Morris's *The Rise of Theodore Roosevelt* (Coward, McCann & Geoghegan, 1979) is an extensive, well-researched biography that follows his career to the death of McKinley. Nathan Miller's *Theodore Roosevelt: A Life* (Morrow, 1992) provides a balanced look at this compelling personality; both his personal and his political lives are examined carefully. *Alice and Edith* by Dorothy C. Wilson (Doubleday, 1989) is a solid joint biography of Roosevelt's two wives. Sylvia J. Morris's *Edith Kermit Roosevelt: Portrait of a First Lady* (Coward, McCann & Geoghegan, 1980) is a richly detailed portrait of the First Lady who redefined the role. (For high school and adult.)

WILLIAM HOWARD TAFT

Bill Severn's *William Howard Taft* (David McKay, 1970) is a well-researched account of his life and times. (For junior high school.)

Lucille Falkof's *William H. Taft* (Garrett Educational Corp., 1990) is a good introductory volume. (For junior and senior high school.)

The Life and Times of William Howard Taft by Henry F. Pringle (Archon Books, 1964) is a comprehensive, two-volume biography. It provides a balanced look at his personal and his political lives. *The Presidency of William Howard Taft* by Paolo E. Coletta (University Press of Kansas, 1973) contains an excellent analysis of his presidency that provides insight into many of the programs he managed to enact. Ishbel Ross's *An American Family: The Tafts, 1678 to 1964* (Greenwood Press, 1977) provides a history of one of the more substantial and influential Ohio families. It concentrates on William Howard Taft, with some discussion of his role as Chief Justice of the Supreme Court. (For high school and adult.)

WOODROW WILSON

Sallie G. Randolph's *Woodrow Wilson, President* (Walker, 1992) provides a great deal of information in a readable manner. (For junior high school.)

J. Perry Leavell's *Woodrow Wilson* (Chelsea House, 1986) is a straightforward and well-written biography. It covers many pivotal events in a clear and concise manner. (For junior and senior high school.)

Woodrow Wilson by August Heckscher (Charles Scribner's Sons, 1991) is an excellent biography that provides a balanced presentation of his personal and his political lives. Thomas J. Knock's *To End All Wars* (Oxford University Press, 1992) concentrates on the World War I era and the political activities, both in the United States and in Europe, that surrounded that war. The definitive biography is Arthur S. Link's *Wilson* (Princeton University Press, 1947–1965), a five-volume masterpiece. Frances W. Saunders's *First Lady Between Two Worlds* (University of North Carolina Press, 1985) is an enjoyable biography of Ellen Axson Wilson, his first wife, who died during his first term. *A President in Love,* edited by Edwin Tribble (Houghton Mifflin, 1981), is a collection of Wilson's letters to Edith Bolling Galt. The letters include comments about the era's current events and show Wilson in a new light, as less aloof and scholarly than his popular image would suggest. *Edith and Woodrow* by Tom Shachtman (G. P. Putnam's Sons, 1981) is a well-done narrative of their courtship and marriage. After Wilson suffered a serious stroke in 1919, many people said that Edith Wilson ran the presidency. (For high school and adult.)

WARREN G. HARDING

Anne Canadeo's *Warren G. Harding* (Garrett Educational Corp., 1990) is a well-done introductory biography with a chronology that places Harding's life and actions in the context of history. (For junior and senior high school.)

Robert K. Murray's *The Harding Era* (University of Minnesota Press, 1969) is a balanced presentation of the achievements and the corruption of Harding's presidency. *The Politics of Normalcy* by Robert K. Murray (Norton, 1973) emphasizes the positive aspects of the Harding presidency such as his basically sensible economic beliefs. *The Shadow of Blooming Grove* by Francis Russell (McGraw-Hill, 1968) is an excellent portrait of "everybody's second choice" at the Republican convention in 1920. (For high school and adult.)

CALVIN COOLIDGE

Rita Stevens's *Calvin Coolidge* (Garrett Educational Corp., 1990) is a good introductory biography. (For junior and senior high school.)

Meet Calvin Coolidge, edited by Edward C. Lathem (Stephen Greene Press, 1960), is a collection of short essays about Coolidge by people who knew him. It provides interesting insights into a basically quiet and unassuming man. Hendrik Booraem's *The Provincial: Calvin Coolidge and His World, 1885–1895* (Bucknell University Press, 1994) is an excellent recounting of his adolescence in late-nineteenth-century rural New England. *Grace Coolidge and Her Era* by Ishbel Ross (Dodd, Mead, 1962) is a well-written biography of Grace Coolidge that describes her lifelong work with the deaf and the hearing-impaired. (For high school and adult.)

HERBERT HOOVER

Suzanne Hilton's *The World of Young Herbert Hoover* (Walker, 1987) is a well-done biography that concentrates on his Quaker childhood. (For junior high school.) David Burner's *Herbert Hoover: A Public Life* (Knopf, 1978) is a comprehensive work. (For junior high school and adult.) Herbert Hoover's *On Growing Up: Letters to American Boys and Girls* (Morrow, 1962) is a unique work for all age levels.

Richard N. Smith's *An Uncommon Man: The Triumph of Herbert Hoover* (Simon & Schuster, 1984) is an excellent, well-balanced biography, highlighting the many accomplishments of his administration. It also discusses the Great Depression. George H. Nash's *The Life of Herbert Hoover: The Engineer 1874–1914* (Norton, 1983) and *The Life of Herbert Hoover: The Humanitarian 1914–1917* (Norton, 1988) are two excellent volumes that deal with Hoover's life before the presidency. (For high school and adult.)

Lou Henry Hoover, Gallant First Lady by Helen B. Pryor (Dodd, Mead, 1969) is a well-done biography of a very interesting woman. (For junior and senior high school.)

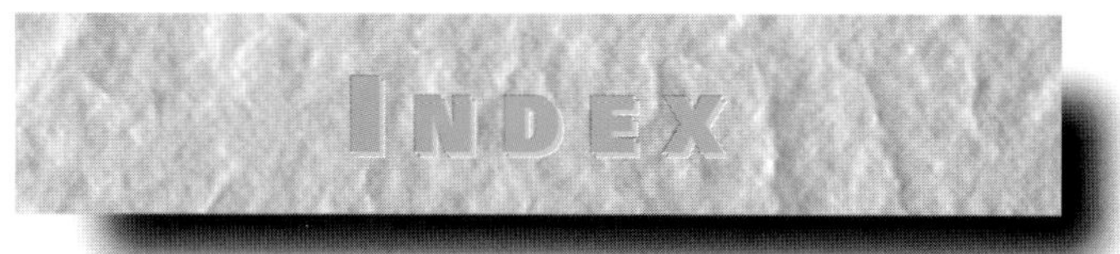

at a glance . . .

President	Volume	President	Volume	President	Volume
George Washington	1	James Buchanan	3	Calvin Coolidge	5
John Adams	1	Abraham Lincoln	3	Herbert Hoover	5
Thomas Jefferson	1	Andrew Johnson	3	Franklin D. Roosevelt	6
James Madison	1	Ulysses S. Grant	3	Harry S. Truman	6
James Monroe	1	Rutherford B. Hayes	4	Dwight D. Eisenhower	6
John Quincy Adams	2	James A. Garfield	4	John F. Kennedy	6
Andrew Jackson	2	Chester A. Arthur	4	Lyndon B. Johnson	6
Martin Van Buren	2	Grover Cleveland	4	Richard M. Nixon	7
William Henry Harrison	2	Benjamin Harrison	4	Gerald R. Ford	7
John Tyler	2	William McKinley	4	Jimmy Carter	7
James K. Polk	2	Theodore Roosevelt	5	Ronald Reagan	7
Zachary Taylor	3	William Howard Taft	5	George Bush	7
Millard Fillmore	3	Woodrow Wilson	5	Bill Clinton	7
Franklin Pierce	3	Warren G. Harding	5		

h

i

j

k

l

m

n

o

p

r

s

t

u

v

w

y

z